And Then . . .

Never Stop Sharing Stories

SCOTT ANTHONY CRAMER

WESTBOW
PRESS®
A DIVISION OF THOMAS NELSON
& ZONDERVAN

WestBow Press books may be ordered through booksellers or by contacting:

WestBow Press
A Division of Thomas Nelson & Zondervan
1663 Liberty Drive
Bloomington, IN 47403
www.westbowpress.com
1 (866) 928-1240

Unless otherwise noted, Scripture is taken from the Holy Bible, New Living Translation, copyright © 1996, 2004, 2015 by Tyndale House Foundation. Used by permission of Tyndale House Publishers, Inc., Carol Stream, Illinois 60188. All rights reserved.

Scripture marked NIV is taken from The Holy Bible, New International Version®, NIV® Copyright © 1973, 1978, 1984, 2011 by Biblica, Inc.® Used by permission. All rights reserved worldwide.

ISBN: 978-1-9736-4483-5 (sc)
ISBN: 978-1-9736-4484-2 (hc)
ISBN: 978-1-9736-4482-8 (e)

Library of Congress Control Number: 2018913361

Print information available on the last page.

WestBow Press rev. date: 11/14/2018

To Cal Rychener,

You rolled the dice on a jerk and in so doing you reflected God's hopeful heart for who His children are becoming. You called me out of the crowd, you shared your stage and gave me a voice. This book doesn't happen without your influence on my life. Period. Thank you.

To Zig Ziglar,

I bumped into him in a church lobby in Texas. When I asked if I could get a picture with him another guy jumped in the photo. Zig leaned toward him. I ended up looking like a photo bomb. But, he shook my hand, looked me in the eye and said, "write a book". While I'm sure he had no idea I flunked college English...twice, and I'm pretty sure he said this to the thousands of people he met each week, those words were fuel when I thought about giving up. The other guy got the photo. I wrote a book. We all miss a great storyteller.

To Northwoods Community Church,

You allowed me to grow up in front of you. You were patient. You were generous. You were gracious. We laughed. We cried. We rolled up our sleeves and went to work together. Heaven is more crowded because of you.

I especially want to thank to Jena Cramer, Carol Cramer, Damon Tomeo and Jackie Bretz for your hours of proofing, correction and encouragement. I could never compensate you for your contribution to this work so I pray eternity will reward you greatly.

Thank you to Chris Banning, Kristen Burkholder, Mark Batterson, Carey Neiuwhof, Erwin McManus, mom, dad and everyone else who I thought I heard say, "write a book." Who'd have thunk it? Certainly not my English professors.

We all have a story. The way in which we write it and share it determines its impact, even long after we are gone. In **And Then...** Scott masterfully describes and demonstrates the power our stories wield. It is a rare find that makes you cry as well as laugh, is theoretical while being intensely practical, and convicts and inspires with equal measure. You will want to read it more than once, and share it, and your own story, with all those for whom you care deeply.

Rocky Rocholl
President, Fellowship of Evangelical Churches

"Scott's heart is all over these pages. He masterfully uses the art of story to inspire his readers to see the hope beyond their pain, provision beyond their inadequacy, and love even in their darkest hours. Everyone has a story and this book will leave you wanting to share yours."

Carey Nieuwhof, Founding Pastor, Connexus Church and author of Didn't See It Coming

"Scott has written a delightful, practical, and helpful book. It reminds us that in a world of soundbites and social media, that it's stories that stick. You will enjoy this book and benefit from it."

Jim Powell
Author, Dirt Matters

Whether you want to change the world, improve your marketing strategy, or simply pass along family stories to future generations, *And Then... Never Stop Sharing Stories* is a must read! As you are taken on a journey with master story teller Scott Cramer you will connect quickly with these relatable and true tales while also having an opportunity to reflect on how to tell a better story, a skill with which we all need to be great!

Damon Tomeo
Head Football Coach, Knox College
Host, Building your Team podcast

Teaching through stories was a method Jesus used. Today we still learn through story telling. Scott has mastered this skill. Not only does he share some of his stories with us but he challenges us to see the stories in our own lives. A read well worth your time and your reflection.

Laura Davis
Preschool director, Connexion, Mt Vernon, Illinois

Scott Cramer's work "And then.." is prophetic, piercing through the cultural fog of the "me generation" all the way down to the temporal marrow of its bones. Tell stories about what we experience like Scott advises, lest our lives become just like fog—burned away and disappearing in the morning sun.

Jackie Bretz
Professor of Journalism, Western Kentucky University

I love it! So natural. So refreshing. Much of the ministry of Jesus was about telling stories and parables. Scott Cramer has done us all a special treat by writing this book.

Dr. Paul Dixon
Chancellor, Cedarville University

"Stories are meant to be shared. I've been fortunate enough to be a part of many stories in Scott Cramer's life. He has an uncanny gift to relate to people and draw out their stories. All people are interesting to Scott. Scott's book will change the way you look at people and their stories. It gives the reader a better appreciation for what people experience and the strength these people get from God. There is hope for all of us. As humans, "And then" should be our rallying cry!"

Jay Burkholder
Principal- Tecumseh Local Schools

Contents

Part Four

And then...ADVENTURE

1

• • •

And Then...

"Create in me a clean heart..."[1] - King David, Psalm 51

When I was a freshman at Galesburg High School in Galesburg, Illinois, the most played song on the cafeteria juke box was, "You Give Love a Bad Name," by Bon Jovi. One day while I was eating lunch, this song was playing in the background. Out of nowhere, a girl runs over, jumps up on our table, and yells "Fight!" Then she jumps from table top to table top to the back of the lunch room.

Finding this announcement irresistible, we all follow her to a circle of people watching a couple of students fighting. But it was not just any fight. It was a girl fight. And not just any girl. Tanya was in this fight. She was tough. She had a wandering eye, so you never knew if she was really looking at you or not. Some of us assumed it was an evolutionary adaptation coming from surviving the roughest neighborhood in town, the one where you were always worried about someone sneaking up on you. No one in his or her right mind messed with Tanya. But for whatever reason on this day, someone did.

There is food everywhere, and the two are punching, scratching, kicking, and pulling hair. And then the other girl picks up a cafeteria tray, and with food flying everywhere, she hits Tanya on the side of her head! Bam! Tanya's eyeball pops out and shoots across the floor. Stunned, everyone freezes as we watch Tanya stop fighting, clutch her face, and chase her eyeball as it rolls under a table.

Teachers escorted all us students out of the lunchroom. As we are standing outside in the hallway, we watch through the big plate glass windows, as our teachers and the cafeteria staff--- on their hands and knees—sort through french fries and peach wedges looking for Tanya's glass eye.

That was a long time ago. But just a few years ago when I told this story to a high school ministry group in Galesburg, a few students came up to me and said a version of this story is still being told at GHS.

We love a good story. We love to listen to stories. We love to tell stories. Stories engage our imagination. Stories can move us to action. They fuel our emotions. Stories can build bridges among multiple generations. I've watched my kids look up from their phones and tablets to listen to their grandpa or grandma tell a story.

Christian minister and futurist Erwin McManus said, "Whoever tells the best story shapes the culture and creates the future."[2] I believe him. I love a good story, but I discovered something else recently. I discovered why I love stories. Two words. I used them in the story about Tanya's surprise. If you're like me, perhaps you've never noticed them before, even though every story has them. My oldest son would say his favorite two words in my stories are "The end." But I suppose, most teenagers would say that about their fathers' stories.

No, these two words are the hinge of every bedtime story you've ever told and every novel you've ever read. A single story usually contains several of these turning points, but there is almost always one primary hinge. Do you know what the two words are?

"And then...."

I love those two words. So simple. Hardly noticeable. In children's books I've noticed the phrase usually begins a sentence at the top of a page somewhere in the middle of the story, after all of the drama has developed. "And then..." makes all the difference in the world.

It's the moment where Scooby-Doo takes the mask off the monster, and the mystery is solved. Or when Apollo Creed can't believe Rocky is getting back up. It's the moment when you've been freezing in the tree stand all day, and then you hear the heavy snap of a twig only to forget you're cold.

"And then..." moments occur when those in danger are rescued and when a serious situation becomes hilarious. "And then..." is when the tension in the story is resolved before "The end" moment arrives.

The longer I live, the more I notice we never seem to confuse an "And then..." moment with a "The end" moment more than when we fail. And we all will fail. Some of us will really blow it.

I believe there are three types of people in this world: those who have blown it, those who are blowing it, and those who will blow it. Nowhere in our lives is it easier to confuse an "And then..." moment with a "The end" moment than when we blow it.

Some of us have already failed. And without knowing how to identify and process an "And then..." moment, we've embraced a "The end" to our story. We may have said, "The end" to a marriage, a ministry, a career or a calling. Or worse, after we've failed again, we've said "The end" to pursuing intimacy with God.

History is full of examples of people who have blown it over the years, whether in Hollywood, major league sports, politics, church leadership or even smaller circles much closer to home. I could name some high-profile people who've blown it, and you would be able to tell me the crime, the words that were spoken, or the dirty deeds that were done.

Some names have even become synonymous with the details of their failure.

Here's one: King David. The Bible has a lot to say about his story, including that he was a good man, possessing an intimacy with God unlike anyone of his day. He was an accomplished shepherd, poet, musician, warrior, and king. And then he blew it. One doesn't need to be too familiar with the inside of a church building to be familiar with the story of David and Bathsheba.

Adultery. Murder. Deceit. Sin after sin. David really blew it. The details are all there in 2 Samuel 11. It's in this chapter, at the end of verse 27 (NIV), we find the biggest understatement in the Bible: "But the thing David had done displeased the Lord."

Ya think? I feel like the Lord is displeased when I miss my devotions two days in a row. David has blown it ---- and big time!

Nathan the prophet tells King David a story one day. It's a story about a poor family and a pet lamb. Because of the moral truth in this story, Nathan tries to get the king to indict himself, and he does. David is broken over his sins. But there are consequences, right? The punishment for adultery is death. The punishment for murder is death. It should be "the end" for David. Instead we see him process an "And then…" moment concerning his serious sins.

What comes next? He owns it. He confesses it. And then he flips it. But God's sentence has been stated, and dire consequences follow.

A baby dies.

A nation cries.

A house divides.[3]

And then, David writes Psalm 51 (NIV) in response. "Create in me a clean heart, oh God, and renew a steadfast spirit within me." David repents and is blessed as he continues to serve God for the remainder of his days.

People will always love stories like this one.

We love stories because we love a good "And then…."

I want to tell you the story someday about the couple who hit a rough patch in their marriage. They both blew it. They separated, resulting in a nasty divorce. "And then…".

I want to hear the story someday of the dad that got off track.

He hurt his wife and abandoned his kids. He blew it. He did and said some things he can never take back, "And then..."

I want to read the story someday about the lady who loved God. She was a good woman, but in a weak moment she made a bad choice. She was hiding her secret for years, paralyzed by fear that someone would find out, but when she finally embraced an "And then...", it freed her soul.

I want the generations that come after me to be motivated and inspired by stories of coaches, business owners, farmers, moms, students, and pastors who have blown it. And then... they allow God to flip it. He uses our stories to bring glory to His name and further His kingdom as long as we are willing to own it and keep sharing the "And then..." of our story.

Oh, the stories that could be told!

Culture-shaping, future-creating stories!

Maybe the reason we feel like we are unable to shape and influence others around us is because we've silenced our story with a "The end" where God wants us to tell the story of our "And then...."

The other day I was lying on my back in the driveway underneath our kayak trailer, rewiring the tail lights. My five-year-old came up to me, and I could see through the corner of my eye that his arms were full of some building materials for another invention he was working on. He says, "Hey dad!"

Without moving I continue to work and ask, "What's up buddy?"

"Did you know the best version of me is still in the future?" he says. Did I mention he's five?

It takes a lot to get this old body to slide out from under something when I'm working. But I scooch my way out and prop up on one elbow, looked him in the eye and ask, "What did you just say?"

In a slightly exhausted voice as if he felt he shouldn't have to repeat himself, he said, "Did you know ... the best version of me... is still in the future?"

I say, "I absolutely believe that, but where did you hear that? Did they teach you that in Sunday school?"

"No, I just know it," he replied.

You may be thinking, "Wow, this kid is so smart! He must have some great parents." Let me also tell you that this is the same kid who, in a crowded movie theater in the front row as I'm trying to get him under control, yells, "You're not my daddy!" Try walking out of a dark movie theater with a toddler yelling that.

But in this moment in the driveway I say to Brady, "Wow. That's pretty deep Brady. Can you tell me more?" He's got my attention now. I'm thinking I'm dealing with a little professor here. I'm ready to take notes.

Instead he says, "Tell you more about what?"

"Well, about this best version of you still being in the future," I say.

"Duct tape, rubber gloves and a magnet," he says. "Where can I find it?" And the conversation was over. I couldn't get him back. He walks away from me towards the garage to continue his search for the supplies.

I don't know if he truly understood what he was saying, or if he was trying to build a time machine to meet the best version of himself. Regardless, my son was speaking truth. There is something about what he said that resonates with my heart, because it's true. God believes that about you as well. Maybe somebody reading this now needs to hear the heart of his or her heavenly Father through the confident voice of a little five-year-old boy.

"Did you know the best version of you is still in the future?"

Don't let the enemy silence you with a "The end" when God has made a way for you to write an "And then…" for your story.

No matter what you've done or where you've been or how old you are, what if the world has yet to see the best version of you?

David blew it. And then…

David and Bathsheba have another son. His name was Solomon. And Solomon was the father of Rehoboam.

And Rehoboam was the father of Abija.

And Abija was the father of Asa.

And on and on, generation after generation all the way to Matthan, who was the father of Jacob, who was the father of Joseph, who was the husband of Mary, the mother of Jesus, the Messiah.[4]

And so the Messiah comes through the line of King David and prophecy is fulfilled.

How's that for an "And then..."? Not to mention the empty tomb. The greatest "And then..." in the history of the world.

What if the best version of you is still in the future? What if the best version of you... isn't you. But it's through you. Through the generations that come after you. Who will tell them the story of your "And then..."?

Remember the quote? "Whoever tells the best story shapes the culture and creates the future."[5]

So, what's your story? Where have you settled for a "The end" in your life? What if instead of settling, "The end" of your story instead becomes the beginning of your greatest "And then..."?

TAKEAWAY

Where have you settled for a "The end" to your story?

Reflect on what might be your greatest "And then...". Write it down.

Part One

. . .

And then...HOPE

2

• • •

90 Seconds

"Whatever happens, my dear brothers and sisters, rejoice in the Lord."
— *The Apostle Paul, Philippians 3:1*

The other night before bed, I gave my wife a kiss goodnight. It was a good one. I reached over to turn off the light on my nightstand, and in my head I'm thinking, "Wow. What a good kiss. I've got to get another one of those." As the room goes dark, I make my return to her, and just before our lips touch she says, "Your beard smells like steak."

"You're welcome," I say seductively.

I then realized she wasn't giving me a compliment. Needless to say there was no more kissing that night!

The smell that made me happy made my wife nauseous.

What makes you happy? There is a kind of happiness I want to try to describe for you. It's a moment of happiness, one I think my wife and I would actually agree upon. In fact, if I could pack it into a vitamin pill, a bottle would be in everyone's medicine cabinet.

I think we've all experienced this kind of happiness, but just in case you haven't, allow me to set it up.

Life can be crazy at our house: seven kids each with their own little messes, lots of muddy boots at the back door, and baskets overflowing with clothes either dirty on the way down to the laundry room or clean on the way back up. We have a big dining room table in our house, and most of the time it's used for homework, experiments, or 4H trash, I mean "crafts."

It doesn't happen every day but there are a few nights a week when we are able to clear off this table and enjoy dinner as a family. But that is not the moment I'm trying to describe. Imagine the nine people in my home seated around this table. I sit at the head of the table closest to the doorway that leads back into the kitchen. My oldest son sits directly on my left, my wife and youngest son are on my right, and the rest of the kids are seated around the table.

Steak from our friend's farm might be on the table, the kind of steak that would make a man's beard smell temptingly delicious. Or there might be pork chops from another friend's farm. Occasionally there might be lamb or chicken or turkey from our own little farm.

The other day there were green beans and potatoes from our garden. We grow those Golden Yukon potatoes. I don't even like vegetables, but when you have to pull that many weeds all summer long, they are delicious! Depending on the time of year there might even be a spinach salad with strawberries from our own strawberry patch.

Can you see it? If you're picturing a Norman Rockwell scene, I haven't done an accurate job of describing this setting. Try this: visualize five different conversations going on at the same time and the baby crying because she doesn't want to sit in a booster seat. Are those feet where my six-year-old's head should be? Yes. "Brady, put your feet down and sit right." Everyone is restless; these bear pups just want to eat. We pray blessing on the food, blessing on the farmers, and we eat. But that's still not the special happiness moment I'm trying to describe.

In an effort to regain some order around the table while we eat, everyone takes turns answering a question. We have this little box of creative and fun questions with questions like, "If you sailed on Noah's ark, which pair of animals would you want to care for?" It's silly and fun and leads to some interesting conversations. But this isn't the moment either.

We are finished eating supper when "the moment" finally arrives.

It is the moment between dinner and dessert.

It only lasts 90 seconds, but I think a book could be written on this moment. I usually push my chair away from the table about eighteen inches and cross my legs while leaning back slightly, knuckles intertwined in front of my top knee cap. This is my post-dinner position.

This moment between dinner and dessert is the 90-second space between being thankful for what I've just experienced and hopeful for what's coming. Don't miss this--it's the small space between thankful and hopeful. There is a smile on my face just thinking about it as I write.

Some of you didn't even know this moment existed let alone know it was so incredible. But now you'll never forget.

Just 90 seconds between dinner and dessert. So simple. So happy. I've noticed it doesn't even matter what was for dinner or what is for dessert. It's the same moment whether it's between crab legs and key lime pie or frozen pizza and an Oreo cookie.

There is something in this space. Oh, if only we could experience this more than a few times a week. If only we could live our life in this moment.

I think we can. I know we should.

We can, because it's simply the mental space and every moment where we find ourselves hanging on to a heart of gratitude with one hand and a hopeful future with the other. We should because no matter what we're going through, the healthiest place to pitch a tent mentally is this moment between thankful for what's now and hopeful for what's next.

It's not just between dinner and dessert. If you look back on your happiest moments in life, you'll find they probably hang between these two adjectives, thankful and hopeful.

This is the 90 seconds after you get back from your honeymoon and you start to settle into your new home. You think back and thank God for blessing you with this person. And now you look to the future with your spouse and begin to dream of all the things God has in store for you.

It is the 90 seconds after a baby is born. You count all the toes and all the fingers. You look at your wife and she is smiling and you think, "How is she smiling after what I just witnessed?" The doctor gives you a thumbs up--everything looks good. In this moment, you're so thankful for God's protection and provision, you can't help but be hopeful for the future of this little life. A tear just formed in the corner of my left eye as I am typing thinking of this moment for all my children, even now, so many years since the birth of our first-born.

I think this is why I love sunsets so much. Sunsets for me are an exponential 90 seconds. Thankful for today…hopeful for tomorrow.

I've watched great leaders, coaches, pastors, fathers and mothers harness the power of this space. I've seen them leverage it with wisdom and grace. Are you having trouble motivating your employees? Teach them how to hold on to the space between thankful and hopeful.

We would be wise to lead our families and our teams into these moments.

I wanted to label this moment. I wanted a word for this moment. I couldn't find one so I tried to invent a word. I couldn't do that either. I wanted something sticky, something easy to remember. All I had was the description of this moment. The space that hung between these two variables, thankful and hopeful, represented the space where I wanted to spend the rest of my life.

Have you ever noticed how the apostles who wrote letters from prison seemed happy in spite of their situation? Ridiculous, unless they knew something about this moment. Maybe they sat in those first century prisons, in this space, between thankful for all that Jesus had done and hopeful for what was to come. One of the greatest testimonies to a lost, hurtful, hateful world is a Christ follower who resides in this space, no matter what.

Several summers ago I received a text from my friend Mack. He and his wife Amber attended the church campus I led at the time. The text read, "Amber was in an accident, I'm heading to the hospital now." I met him at the ER and his wife was ok. They had her hooked up to all this medical stuff, and monitors were making sure everything was ok.

I prayed with them. I was the pastor in the room.

In those moments I try to stand a little straighter. I try to be a little taller. I don't know why.

Mack showed me pictures of the car. Unreal. It was a scorched and wrinkled pile of metal. A stranger pulled Amber out just before the engine exploded and caught the car on fire. We thanked God she survived.

Now, lying in the emergency room, Amber continued to cry uncontrollably because her friend Nichole, who was in the car with her, had been life-flighted to the Neuro-ICU in a nearby city with possible brain damage. These ladies were both nurses who were on their way to help a friend.

I wouldn't want to be a nurse and be required to work on another nurse. They know too much. Such was the case with Amber. As a nurse, she'd observed every symptom in the moments between the crash and the ambulance arriving. Now lying in an emergency room bed, she had played out the worst-case scenario.

As it turned out, it was as bad as Amber had diagnosed. Doctors communicated the prognosis to Justin, Nichole's husband. If Nichole lived, there was high probability of brain damage. Nichole was in rough shape, unresponsive.

Justin and Nichole didn't attend my church, but they were faithful to another great church in town, and I considered Justin a friend. I happened to be going right by the hospital one day, and I thought maybe I would just quickly run up and pray for her.

A few days had passed with no real improvement for Nichole. Justin and Nicole's church had just hired a new pastor, and I remember thinking, "I don't want step on his toes. This is kind of outside of my jurisdiction." I decided to go in, trying not to draw any attention to myself. I hoped to just give Justin a hug, pray for Nichole and leave.

I walked into the waiting room, and right away, I'm startled by a "Hey Scott!" It was Justin. I give him a hug, tell him how sorry we were and that I just wanted to come up and pray for his wife if he would let me.

He lets me go back to her room as he stays in the waiting room with friends and family. Doctors have Nichole hooked up to all these machines, and I don't know if she was in a coma or an induced coma to prevent brain swelling. I don't remember all the details, but I do know in this moment Justin didn't know if his wife was going to live at all or live but need machines to help…with whatever. The machines beep. I can hear air pumping through tubes. I'm supposed to be praying, instead I'm staring, thinking, "What if this were you, Scott? What would you do if the very person you found most precious on this earth were hooked up to all these machines? How would you respond?"

I pray for her.

I pray for him.

I pray for me.

I return to the waiting area, and he's still surrounded by friends and family with more people coming in by the minute. I just want to get out of there.

Justin is the only one in the room sitting up straight. And when he stands up to hug a new visitor, he's like a foot taller than everyone. I'm 6'-3" in my work boots and in my memory of this moment, he stood a few inches taller than I did.

I asked him the other day. He's 5'-9". Nothing against guys who are 5'-9", it's just not normal for me to feel shorter than someone who is not...tall. This day, I did.

In the hospital, I noticed he was the one ministering to everyone else. I was the pastor in the room and he was ministering to me! I said, "Justin, you...are...an oak. How are you so composed with so much uncertainty?"

And then, I'll never forget what he said, without missing a beat, "Scott, I gave Nicole to Jesus a long time ago. Whether she lives or not...she belongs to Him."

Those words have spoken a thousand sermons to my soul since. I'm not sure I'm there yet, but I think I'm starting to get it.

Justin's secret? He was rooted in the space between "thankful" and "hopeful." Ninety seconds.

Justin was thankful for all that God had blessed him with up until that point. And regardless of the outcome, he was hopeful for Nichole's prognosis here on earth or her eternity with Jesus. That's attractive Christianity.

I have an idea. Instead of picking fights on social media, let's try getting rooted in this "90 seconds." I believe it's only a Christ-follower who can reside in that space long term, no matter what life throws our way. It's only a follower of Jesus who can truly hang onto thankfulness for what He did on the cross along with a hope for what eternity will bring in the future. No one else can really be rooted in this space.

At any stage of life, at any age, whether at the edge of the unknown or the verge of death's doorstep, no matter what the doctors say, even when the test results come back positive, we can live in that 90 seconds between being thankful for what Jesus has done for us and hopeful for what the future holds.

I cross paths with Mack and Amber occasionally, a beautiful family blessed by God. Just recently I saw Justin and Nichole at a Mexican restaurant. God had answered our prayers with her full recovery. I stopped by their table on my way out and said hello. As I walked away I thanked God again for their inspiring faith and the living example of how to live in the 90-second space between thankful and hopeful.

If we're lucky, we'll get ninety years on this earth. I wish I could live it with my beard smelling like steak and my wife wanting to kiss me anyway. Instead I'm going to spend it rooted in a continual 90-second space between thankful and hopeful.

Will you join me?

TAKEAWAY:

Take a moment and list some people, experiences or things you are thankful for. For what are you hopeful and why?

What distractions are keeping you from living your life in this 90-second space between thankful and hopeful?

3

• • •

Sweet Silence

*"Jesus loved Martha and her sister and Lazarus. Yet
when he heard that Lazarus was sick, he stayed where
he was two more days." John 11:5-6*

Wait. What? That can't be right. Read the above verse again.
Shouldn't it say, "Jesus loved Martha and her sister and Lazarus so
he got up and left at once and went and healed him."? These sisters
are expecting to see Jesus, or at least a message indicating he's on his
way: "Dear sisters, I'll be there soon!" -Jesus

Instead, nothing. No reply. Only silence quietly fertilizing the
growing resentment in their hearts.

There are times that it is quiet. Somewhere my wife is reading
this, puzzled and scratching her head. She knows I can't be talking
about the noise level in our house. Instead, I'm referring to my
conversations with God. And I shouldn't say "quiet," because I'm
still talking. But in my conversations with God, I'm often met with
silence.

As I look back through years of prayer journals, the "silent seasons" are easy to recognize. I pray for work, church, community, family, neighbors, adoption...the same requests over and over. Voicing the same concerns. God's response? Silence.

I begin to analyze everything. Is there something wrong with my request? Is there something wrong with me? Am I really listening to God? Am I not praying the right way? Should I fast? Should I fast longer?

Moments after the resurrection, Mary Magdalene, weeping and confused, is asking for the dead body of Jesus. Who is she asking? The living Jesus! Did he give her what she wanted? No, thankfully. If we understood how limited our vision is in comparison to how big God's plan is, we would see that His silence is good.

Silence requires trust. He deserves it.

Jesus has a friend named Lazarus and he's ill...like going to die, and so his sisters Mary and Martha send word to Jesus to say, "Lord, the one you love is sick." These sisters know what Jesus can do. He's healed the sick before and these sisters have seen it. This would be a slam-dunk for Jesus. This isn't just anyone--this is his friend.

But instead of an answer, there is this silence.

Lazarus dies. And by the time Jesus gets there, Lazarus has been dead for four days. Four days.

When pragmatic Martha heard that Jesus was coming, she went out to meet him--but Mary stayed at home. "Lord," Martha said to Jesus, "If you had been here, my brother would not have died"[6], John 11:20.

At this point, I'm with Martha on this. "Tell him Martha: 'Jesus, I know you are to be about your Father's business. But in my family business, we show up on time!'"

Jesus tells them to remove the heavy stone from the tomb. Reluctantly, they do it.

And then...Jesus raises Lazarus from the dead.

"Lazarus come out!", Jesus called in a loud voice. The dead man came out, his hands and feet wrapped with strips of linen, and a cloth around his face. Jesus said to them, "Take off the grave clothes and let him go."

Did Mary and Martha get Lazarus back? Yes. They get even more. Instead of Mary and Martha experiencing Jesus as healer like they had asked, they get to experience Jesus Christ as the Resurrection and the Life. Wow. I love that! I think the devil cringes when we understand this.

There is a different ending to the story, however, if his sister gets her prayer answered. If Jesus hurries to Lazarus' side and he is healed, that's nice. Instead, Mary and Martha (and don't forget Lazarus) experience silence, "and then..." they experience Jesus' resurrection power.

Because Jesus loved them, he trusted them with His silence.

What if the silence you're experiencing is a sign of God's love? What if He's trusting you with His silence? Does that understanding change anything? Absolutely! He has not forgotten about you. He trusts you with the grace of his silence.

He loves you.

In his book "Keeping Hope Alive," the late Christian author and professor Lewis Smedes writes:

Waiting is our destiny as creatures who cannot by themselves bring about what they hope for. We wait in the darkness for a flame we cannot light, we wait in fear for a happy ending we cannot write. We wait for a not yet that feels like a not ever. Waiting is the hardest work of hope.[7]

"Waiting... is the hardest work... of hope."

Keep waiting.

Keep hoping.

If God just gave us what we asked for, He wouldn't be able to do more than we can imagine.

TAKEAWAY:

Where do you feel like you're waiting for God to show up in your life?

How does it change things if you knew God was trusting you with His silence?

4

• • •

Road Kill

"For I know the plans I have for you," says the Lord,
"They are plans for good and not for disaster, to give
you a future and a hope." Jeremiah 29:11

I come from a long line of hunters, trappers and farmers. In my branch of the family tree, I've got four sons. We "Cramer men" are typical. We like guns and hunting and boxing and guts and gore. Boys to the core! When I see road kill, I automatically think about the value of the pelt.

Confession time. I think road kill is cool. I know, I have issues. But when I'm driving down the road whether alone or with my family, we play a little game. Who can identify the road kill first? We all see the pile of fur way up in the distance…then someone will shout, "coyote!" or "raccoon!" Sometimes it's more of a question. We'll actually drive by the mangled mess, look at each other, and hazard a guess …. "possum"? The first person to correctly identify the species wins. It's a game. It's gross. We like it.

One Sunday morning I was on my way to church from our home

in the country, and as I was on the highway, I saw something along the side of the roadway up in the distance that caught my attention.

As I got closer I realized that it might be some sort of road kill, maybe a raccoon or coyote...could it be perhaps...a turtle? It was. This thing was huge! It was flipped over, upside down with the top of his head resting on the pavement. I was amazed at the size of this turtle. I drove past and I had this thought, "I wonder if it's still alive, and it's just tired from trying to get back on its feet?" I mean it's not an impossibility, right? A turtle could get hit by a car and knocked into a position it can't really get itself out of. It might try all night and just become exhausted. And then, with this kind of thinking and compassion, I turned around to see if maybe this turtle wasn't actually dead but just needed a little help.

Life can be like that. Somewhere on the road to your dreams and visions for your future, you feel like you got hit by a truck. The hit could come in the form of a discouraging word from a close friend, an interview that didn't pan out, or a relationship that hit a rough patch. And at fifty-five mph your dreams look dead. Your road to success looks more like road kill. But maybe it's not--maybe you just need a little encouragement, someone to turn the car around and take the time to speak hope and life and truth into your situation.

Maybe you're reading this now and you'd say, "Scott, you just described my life with the word picture of a road kill turtle!" If so, then Jeremiah 29:11 is for you, "For I know the plans I have for you," says the LORD. "They are plans for good and not for disaster, to give you a future and a hope."

You may be wondering what happened to the turtle. I'd rather not say. But don't worry, God has a better plan for you. Wipe the tire marks off of that dream and pursue it. And don't forget to stop, turn around and encourage a few others along the way.

TAKEAWAY

What's the dream you've allowed to die on the roadside of "Life"?

What's one thing you could do today to breathe life back into this crushed dream?

Who could you encourage today?

5

• • •

Sparkle

"Don't worry about anything; instead, pray...then you'll experience God's peace."
- *The Apostle Paul, Philippians 4:6-7*

"Daddy...your eyes don't sparkle."

You can fool a lot of people, but not a three-year-old. My son was right--I had truly lost my "sparkle."

"God help me," I said just under my breath as he skipped away, leaving me to my thoughts.

Less than a year before, our community and the church I led hit a rough patch like nothing I had ever experienced before. Because it was a season of one tragedy after another, my staff and I could barely catch our breath.

The hurt, the pain, sickness and even death drained us.

An eight-year-old boy was diagnosed with cancer.

A fourteen-year-old was hit by a truck while riding his bike and killed.

A twenty-one-year-old man was killed in a car accident.

Two sixteen-year-old girls from our city were killed in a car crash after a football game.

A mother enters the delivery room with the excitement of a perfect pregnancy up to that point. Something goes wrong. After they put her under to do an emergency C-section, she wakes up three days later in ICU with a hysterectomy and news of her infant son's death.

My job as a pastor was to deliver a message of hope into our community each weekend. Yet each tragic situation was met with a part of my own hope chewed on and chipped away by the grief and sadness experienced as I walked with each family the best I could. Then there were additional burdens I had to carry alone as the senior staff member: stories of abuse, rape, and trauma.

I tried to teach myself how to not flinch. Someone would come into my office, and as soon as I began to sense the conversation heading toward a confession or a revelation of some deep wound, I would tell myself, "Just don't flinch Scott. Don't let any visible sign of disgust or shock hit your face. Act like you have heard this before. Jesus has. Love them like Jesus." When I would lay my head on my pillow at night, the details of abuses were so disgusting, I pleaded with God to wash my brain. Sometimes He did.

Often my staff and I would hang out up front in the office lobby area at the end of a day. We would have informal discussions, brainstorming sessions, debates... Nerf football. During one such occasion, our youth pastor Andrew received a text. We all heard his phone "ding." No one thought anything of it. I continued to teach my staff how to perfect a curve ball with a wiffleball down the hallway. After looking at his phone, he said, "Oh no." We all stopped.

"A school on Main Street is on lockdown. Active shooter situation one block from the school. Sounds like a potential murder/suicide situation," he said.

"Really? Right now?" I said with obvious doubt in my tone. "And you know this through a text?" I didn't believe it.

It was true. Andrew's sister was sitting in a salon chair while her hairdresser was getting texts of the unfolding events. The hairdresser's friend happened to be a neighbor to the scene of the crime and was standing on her front porch watching it happen. We were literally getting information from an eyewitness before the police had time to ask questions. It was surreal.

I remember saying, "Just tell me it doesn't involve any of our people. Please, tell me it's not someone who goes to our church."

Andrew texted. Then waited. Then spoke.

The names were familiar. They included our people. "I can't do this," I thought with such resonance it felt like I had said it out loud. I hadn't, but I felt a physical heaviness on my chest. This new burden literally weighed me down and forced me to sit on the windowsill as I stared out the church's storefront window.

The shooter was one of the nicest people I had met. What a strange sentence to see typed onto the page. A big guy, he walked with a cane because of the damage to his knees from the years working in his specific industry. He was a handsome guy who always wore a baseball cap. A barrel of a man, he was almost as wide as he was tall, and when he smiled his eyes disappeared. It was a great smile. So much so that when he asked to volunteer at our church, we put him as a greeter at one of our front doors. He'd lean his cane against the doorjamb and smile that smile as he greeted guests every third Sunday of the month.

But gripped by bitterness, anxiety and a darkness I had never seen or noticed, he shot and killed his soon to be ex-wife during an argument. His mother who happened to be there helping him move out watched from the front porch. "He immediately realized what he had done. It was like he woke up. His expression changed from anger to fear. He then put the gun to his chest and pulled the trigger...readjusted the angle of the barrel and pulled the trigger again", she said.

I hadn't met this man's son until he asked if I would do his dad's funeral. Article after article came out in the newspaper. Back-to-back funerals, with simultaneous visitations in separate parts of the building. Never had I experienced such tension, confusion and grief. We did our best to walk alongside the kids and the rest of the family. It was God himself that carried me through certainly one of the most difficult funerals I have ever been a part of.

Then there was the graveside service. It was packed. After this service, we usually allow the family to stay as long they need. I typically try to connect with family members sitting in the front with a handshake or a hug and let them know I'm praying for them. Then I step back into the background.

On this day, I stood far away, a hundred scattered tombstones between me and the blue tent full of people.

A man I didn't recognize came up to me. He was in his mid-fifties and had a weathered face, but I remember something so gentle about his countenance. There was something about his eyes. This is hard to explain, but before he spoke a word, I wanted to be his friend--I wanted to get to know him. He says, "Hey, great job pastor. That couldn't have been easy. Thank you for your message of hope. I know exactly what this family is going through."

Are you kidding me? I thought. "How?" I said with obvious disbelief. He said, "My father shot and killed my mother, my sister and my brother...then himself. I was 12 and wasn't home at the time."

What do you say? I was stunned. "I'm so sorry," I said. Then I asked him his name. When he told me, I remembered it sounded familiar. He told me why. He said, "My daughter was one of the sixteen-year-olds killed a few weeks ago."

I thought, how is this man here right now? How is he even standing let alone looking so peaceful? You know what stood out to me the most about this man? What struck me most was despite everything he had been through in his past and as recently as two weeks before, his eyes sparkled. He was the embodiment of God's peace.

"Then you will experience God's peace, which exceeds anything we can understand..."⁸ Philippians 4:7a. God's peace in this man didn't make sense to me. And then, I recognized how much I wanted God's peace and how desperately the world needs it.

I learned that day God's peace is not simply the absence of storms. It's a peace exceeding all understanding because it's in the middle of life's storms where you find it. This man told me just a little about his faith in Jesus Christ and that God's peace alone had been his anchor through it all. I pointed back to the blue tent and said, "The son who's lost his parents needs you to walk with him. No one can introduce him to the reality of God's peace like you can."

I went home that night and took a long walk with Jesus. I asked a lot of hard questions. Did I miss something? Were there any warning signs I should have noticed? Could I have prevented this?

Nothing. Just a thousand-yard stare.

My son Brady, only three years old, took my face in his hands and just stared at me. So seriously, he put his face just inches away from mine. I watched his eyes dart from left to right. I could tell he was looking at one eye, then the other and back again. I was struck by the concern on his face. Looking deep into my eyes he said, "Daddy...your eyes don't sparkle."

And then, I remember writing this in my prayer journal later in the evening: "A man left to his thoughts alone is doomed. I must hear from God every day."

I don't know if I've got it all figured out, but I'm getting there. I'm getting my sparkle back. It all starts with a daily surrender of my worry and anxiety, embracing a thankful heart while focusing on the hope I have in Jesus' promise of His peace.

I don't know what you're going through today, but can I encourage you? Don't worry about anything; instead, pray about everything. Tell God what you need and thank him for all he has done. Paul the Apostle writes: "Then you will experience God's peace, which exceeds anything we can understand. His peace will guard your hearts and minds as you live in Christ Jesus" Philippians 4:7.

TAKEAWAY:

What are some things you've been carrying that have stolen your sparkle?

What are you doing to hear from God every day?

6

• • •

Imaginary Sharks

"In peace I will lie down and sleep, for you alone, Lord, make me dwell in safety."[9] *–David Psalm 4:8*

When I was too young to understand the difference between make believe and reality, my parents took me with them to see the movie "Jaws." I was five years old when they decided to go to a drive-in showing of this 1975 Steven Spielberg classic. I don't blame my parents for much, but I do blame them for my fear of sharks. They had a 1970's Honda Civic. To their credit they had laid the back seat down and brought my blanket and pillow, and they thought I would sleep through the late show, but I didn't. I saw it all. I heard the soundtrack. I saw the bloody water.

To make matters worse we moved to the East Coast not long after this cinematic encounter with "Jaws". In fact, we moved to the New England area, which is the movie's setting. When it came time for little Scotty to take swimming lessons, it was in the ocean. If not in the ocean, it was in a lake or a pond. But in my young mind and unable to swim, it was always in the ocean to me.

All of us little kids would wade out into the water up to our belly buttons with our instructor, and she would have us make a circle while holding hands. To help us learn how to go underwater, she would have us play "Ring Around the Rosy." When we would get to the "ashes, ashes we all fall...down," we were all supposed to go under water. We all did, except one. Me. I was certain as soon as I put my head under water, I'd hear the infamous sound track and Jaws would eat me. I could almost see the blood in the water. So, I would just let everybody else go under water, including the instructor, and when they came back up, I'd pretend like I was coming back up for air. I'd splash water on my face and in my hair, all smiles. Nobody said anything. I thought I had them fooled.

One day while doing our opening exercise of "Ring Around the Rosy," when everyone went down under water, I was surprised to find there were two of us standing up: the instructor and me, directly across from each other. She had that look and I knew exactly what she was thinking. It was almost like I could read her mind. I'm sure she was thinking, "You've seen the movie too!"

If you were to ask my wife or my mom or most of my extended family, "Where is the most peaceful place on earth.... If you could go anywhere to find peace, where would you go?" They would tell you, "The beach. The ocean waves crashing on the sand are so relaxing." My brother in-law's family would say "Riding the waves and the smell of salt water."

And I would disagree with them because while those things might be true, they seem to forget something. There are sharks in there and they want to eat you!

I believe this is why God gave us the Great Lakes. There are no sharks in Lake Michigan. No nasty saltwater. If you want to feel like you're on the West coast, take a vacation to Michigan. If you want to feel like you're on the East coast, find a place in Wisconsin. Believe me, your kids will never know...at least for a few years.

You might say, "Scott, your fear is unjustified." My kids would say, "Dad, the odds are better you'd be bitten by a person in New

York City than by a shark in the ocean." We would all agree and say, "Fear is stealing my peace." And you are right.

When my youngest son, Brady, was four years old, he would often get scared at night. He would come down and sleep in our room. Bringing his blanket and his pillow, he would lie on the floor next to my side and whisper, "Dad. Dad. Dad...Daddy... I'm scared. Will you hold my hand?" As he is lying on the floor, I would have to contort my body so that I could reach down from my bed and hold his hand.

As I did, I would actually feel the anxiety in his soft little four-year-old hand. There were times I thought I could feel his heartbeat through his fingertips. But in less than ten seconds, I could feel his hand begin to relax. Within a few minutes, he would let go. Then I would gently lay his hand on his chest as he slept in peace.

What Brady experienced in this moment was the "Peace of Daddy." Brady experienced the inward tranquility of a mind grounded in the nearness of his daddy's presence, his daddy's promise, and his daddy's power. Brady understands his daddy's presence, my ability to be physically near him. Sometimes that was not enough. He wanted to hold my hand, to be in contact with me.

My son understands his daddy's promise. He knows my heart for him. He knows I'm for him and not against him. I'm not going to trick him. He knows I'm not going to do anything that would hurt him. I'm not going to scare him. There's a reason he doesn't go to his brothers. He knows his daddy's heart is for his good.

Brady is confident in his daddy's power. He believes I have the ability to take out the boogey man. In his mind I'm bigger and more powerful than any threat in the darkness of the night, whether in his dreams or in our home.

This is how it is for the Christ follower when it comes to the "Peace of God."

No matter what sharks are circling us at this moment...whether real or imaginary, we can experience the "Peace of God." We can experience the inward tranquility of a mind grounded in the nearness of our heavenly Father's presence, promise and power.

TAKEAWAY:

Identify the imaginary sharks in your life right now that are stealing your peace.

What would it look like to allow God to hold your hand through this season?

Part Two

• • •

And then...PROVISION

7

• • •

Creekin' Shoes

"This means that anyone who belongs to Christ has become a new person!"
                    —*The Apostle Paul, 2 Corinthians 5:17a*

"Do you own a pair of creekin' shoes?" I asked an auditorium full of people for a show of hands to this question, and I was surprised by how few said they did. I thought everyone had a pair of creekin' shoes. Growing up on the banks of Court Creek and canoeing down the Spoon River, creekin' shoes are a must. You can't drag a canoe out of the muddy Spoon River in flip flops. And you wouldn't dare go barefoot because of the glass and metal that would slice your feet.

Creekin' shoes are the last destination in the lifespan of tennis shoes in our house right before the trash. Creekin' shoes smell terrible. Some strange combination of sewer and dead rodent. We keep our family's creekin' shoes in the garage. They don't come inside with the everyday shoes. Creekin' shoes are not worthless; they are just worth...less. And all creekin' shoes got their start as brand new sneakers. Remember when they were brand new? You've done this. You used them just for the good stuff. School, church, maybe even carry them into the gym in your duffle bag. You took good care of them but eventually, they start showing a little wear. All of a sudden, you are not afraid to wear them in the rain.

Then one day you look down and realize you're wearing them while mowing the grass. Oh well. They aren't worthless, but they've gradually become worth…less. Before you know it, you're painting the garage in them because it doesn't matter if you spill some paint on them. With each stage in the life cycle of shoes at our house, they are gradually becoming worth…less. Then one day you decide to hit the river with some friends, and you've got yourself some creekin' shoes.

Oh, the subtle slip from "favored" to "forsaken" in the lifespan of a pair of shoes.

So it is with our lives.

We aren't as shiny as the other people we see around town, sipping mochas at the coffee shop or walking into church. We are tempted to think, because of the things we've done in the past, that somehow we are "worth… less." And without even knowing it, some of us begin to settle for "creekin' shoe faith." Eventually we don't even think it's worth the effort to keep our heart and mind clean anymore, let alone that God could still use us to impact the world.

We have blown it so many times, falling for that same old temptation, that same old sin. In our mind, our purpose and place on this Earth is at the bottom of the shoe life cycle. All there is to do now is wait for Jesus to come back. I know, I know, the Bible tells us we aren't worthless. We learned that in Sunday school. However, you'd have a hard time convincing some of us that we aren't "worth…less".

If that's you, you've let your guard down, and you're going to lose the battle for your heart. You've embraced a future for your heart that contradicts God's heart for your future.

And then, think of this: you and I have an enemy who recognizes your eternal potential. Your Kingdom potential. You were made on purpose, for a purpose. And your purpose is a means to an end that all of us share: to bring God glory and further His kingdom here on earth. We have an enemy who understands this. Maybe even more than we do. We actually see an example of this in scripture.

There is a moment with Jesus recorded in Luke 22 where Jesus says, "Simon, Simon, Satan has asked to sift each of you like wheat. But I have prayed for you..." This passage is fascinating because at this point Peter hasn't done anything! He hasn't written any books. He hasn't preached any sermons. Yet even Satan recognizes Peter's potential before anyone else does, even Peter! Satan asks for permission to take him out.

What if the enemy attacks us at the very place God has gifted us? What if the place of our biggest struggle is the very place God wants to partner with us to make the biggest impact in this world!? If this is true, this battle is a big deal! It also confirms you and I have a role to play in advancing the Kingdom.

Understanding this changes everything.

God doesn't just use creekin' shoes sometimes. He loves creekin' shoes. So much so, He brings creekin' shoes into his house and wears them to do His greatest work.

TAKEAWAY:

Where have you settled for this "Creekin' Shoe" faith in your life?

Are you embracing a future for your heart that contradicts God's heart for your future?

8

• • •

Thin Ice

"The way of a fool is right in his own eyes, but he who heeds counsel is wise."
— *King Solomon, Proverbs 12:15*

The first time I heard my neighbor talk about shed hunting, I thought it meant he was shopping for a tool shed. Every year deer shed their antlers in late winter and then they grow back in the summer. So sometime between late February and early April, my boys and I go hunting for these antler sheds. They can be found in fields and timber where deer eat, bed down, and travel. However, if you wait too long to find them, the mice and squirrels will actually eat these antler sheds.

A few years ago I took my boys out after the snow finally started melting. I just knew the receding snow might reveal some of these antler sheds. We had been hunting my dad's property the previous fall and had seen a nice buck. He was brute! He had a nice tall rack. And he had a little orange patch of fur on top of his head right between his antlers. We named him Carrot Top.

This particular parcel of land is only about thirty-three acres, but it is prime pass through territory for big deer. We arrived at the property on this day only to find the creek was flooded. In the middle of my dad's land is Haw Creek. It divides the north side of the property from the south. On the south side of the creek is where the deer are, along with timber and food plots. Our deer stands and most of our trail cameras are placed on the south side of the creek as well, but the north side is the only way to access this property.

Try to visualize this creek. If you were to stand in the middle of the water, it would be three or four feet deep at the most. The banks of the ravine would be about eight to ten feet up to the edge of the fields. This creek is fifteen to thirty feet wide, from top edge to top edge.

There is a low water bridge in one spot, which you can just walk or drive across and barely get your boots wet.

But, on this day with the snow melting and the spring thaw in full affect, the water was all the way up to about a foot from cresting over the top. Do the math, about ten to fourteen feet deep of moving water. Not a creek anymore. It's a river. A lot of water, moving really fast. It was deceiving because big ice chunks had broken loose and then got dammed up to the downstream side of the property.

I'm talking ice chunks big enough to be Tom Sawyer's raft. Eight inches thick and four to six feet square. My three oldest boys who at the time, were fourteen, ten and eight, and myself need to get across this "creek."

As all good stories start, "Boys," I said, "watch this. I'm going to jump onto these big pieces of ice from one to the next. Wait until I get to the other side and then you follow me one at a time, jumping exactly where I do."

I hop out on the first one. As I land my weight jostles the raft-like ice and I immediately put both arms out in an effort to balance myself on the wobbling sheet of ice. I jumped to the next and then the next, finally leaping up on to the bank.

I turn around and my boys are already doing the same thing. I think to myself, "Who said I'm not fun? I am such an adventurous dad. These boys are so lucky. They'll tell their kids someday how cool I was."

We walked that timber for hours. Most of the land on the south side of the creek was on the north side of the ridge, which meant the snow hadn't melted yet due to the long shadows cast by the winter sun staying so low. So, with big steps with heavy boots crunching through the icy layer and into the deep snow, we climbed to the top of the ridge continuing to look for antler sheds. We zigzagged the whole property all in a row about twenty feet apart so as not to miss anything. Hours of tromping. Nothing.

We were exhausted. My boys were troopers, soldiering up for the whole experience. They were loving it. I need to mention they are survival experts. They've read all the books on how to survive. They can make fish hooks out of bird bones. They know what bugs you can eat. They can tell how long you have after a rattlesnake bite before you die. If you're ever on an airplane that crash lands in the wilderness, you want one of my boys with you. They are enjoying this whole experience but they are pooped.

No antler sheds. We call it a day. We head back to the truck and we get to the creek, and guess what? The ice has shifted. Now, instead of raft-size sheets of ice, there are much smaller pieces. I can see now just how quickly the water is moving underneath it. It's intimidating! So we walk another mile of the creek looking for a place where we can cross on chunks of ice.

I find a spot. But this time the pieces of ice were about half the size compared to what we had crossed before. I had to try.

I said, "Boys, let me go first." My oldest son Sky, says, "Dad, give me your phone. I want to get a video of this."

"No way!" I said and then half-joking, "I'm not going to let you get my death on video!"

I begin to cross that creek and I get to about three feet from the other side, and all of the sudden, "shkaloonk" (that's the sound a 240-pound man makes when he pencil dives into icy water), I go down. I lunge toward the bank. Instantly I'm up to my chest in freezing cold water, and my hands are grasping for anything to hold on the muddy bank. The bank is covered with a thin layer of ice no thicker than the glaze on a donut. The crackling ice feels like razor blades on my fingers as each grasp digs into the muddy bank. I'm only able to use my upper-body strength as I can't touch the bottom. The water is pulling me down stream, and then I'm able to finally grab some small saplings, but I'm struggling. I'm actually panicking because it takes hardly any time at all before I can't feel my legs. I think I'm moving them but I'm not making any progress. I'm scared. Falling through ice is a terrifying experience.

Just then, one of my survival experts calls out in a calm voice from the other bank, "Dad, you have fifteen minutes until you die!"

I remember this thought going through my mind, for real, "Do I spend my final fifteen minutes trying to get out of this creek or do I just turn around and give my boys some final wisdom before I leave this world?" Realizing I wasn't in a very credible position to deliver any type of wisdom, I continued to pull myself up to safety.

Long story a little bit shorter, obviously, I was able to get out of the creek because you're reading this today. I told the boys to head south. It would be a long trek and they were already exhausted, but there wasn't an alternative. If they just stayed on a southern course, they would run right into a certain farmer's land where they would then see the farmer's house. It would be several miles of rugged terrain but I'd be waiting there with the truck.

Now, the first thing my young survival experts taught me about falling through the ice is the importance of getting warm. And this doesn't happen wearing wet clothing. Believing I had only minutes to live due to hypothermia, as soon as I got to the truck, I turned on the heat and stripped off all of wet clothing and drove across the countryside to wait for my boys at the farmer's house.

I arrive at the rendezvous point and decide to drive back by their machine shed so I can get a good view of the horizon from which my boys should be coming. I wait and wait. I begin to worry. But my worry is interrupted by the sound of a screen door slamming. I look in the rearview mirror towards the house and it's the farmer's wife. I look down and think, "Uh oh." Not only was I a trespassing stranger. I'm sitting in my truck in my underwear! Another story for another time.

The boys finally make it, and we're headed home, and then, I start thinking, "what if I'd made it across the creek and then one of my boys had fallen in while following my example?" I'm almost certain it would have ended tragically. Here, I'm setting an example for my boys. I'm supposed to be getting smarter as I get older. That was so stupid! How could I have not seen that coming?

As we're driving, I turned to them and I said, "Boys, please don't ever do anything like that. I'm sorry. I'm embarrassed to say that is one of the three most foolish things I've ever done in my life."

Then my youngest pipes up from the backseat and asks in a chipper voice, "What are the other two, daddy?"

I said, "Boy, you will never know this side of heaven."

I'll bet as you read about this icy creek, at the first opportunity we had to cross it, you could have finished the story differently. Am I right? You could see it in your mind and thought, "Don't you cross that creek!"

You could see the danger in the story and you weren't even there. Why couldn't I see it at the time? I had too much emotion invested in deer antlers! I didn't want to miss ole' Carrot Top's rack!

If you ever find yourself asking, "Why didn't I see this coming?" Guess what? Somebody did. And you didn't ask them. And they didn't tell you because they think you wouldn't have listened!

I wonder how many times we ignore the danger of thin ice in pursuit of our desires. We'd be wise to heed the wisdom of those on the opposite bank who can see the danger before us.

The best way to avoid hearing, "How did you not see that coming?" about our decisions is to ask others, "What do you see?" before we decide.

TAKEAWAY

Describe a time where you look back and think, "How did I not see that coming?"

What did you learn and what wisdom would you pass on to the next generation?

9

• • •

Beans, Bait & Bells

"And my God will meet all your needs..."[10] – The Apostle Paul while in prison, Philippians 4:19

When I was a kid, my dad once took my brother and me on a fishing trip. Half of the fun of a trip like this was the preparation. I'm sure you know what it's like as you get everything ready--pack the tent, cooking gear and fishing poles. You have all the mental images of what this expedition is going to be like. This visualizing keeps you motivated and excited for weeks leading up to the trip.

My brother and I talked about how we were going to live off the land. We were only going to eat what we caught. We'd have fish for breakfast, lunch and dinner. It was going to be awesome! To guarantee success for our future meals, we packed our favorite bait and lures. My Grandpa on my dad's side used to make his own dip bait for catfish. Dip bait is some nasty smelling, sticky stuff. It looks like a jar of peanut butter but it smells like pig poop.

Grandpa Cramer was a big man who I'd never seen wear anything but old denim bib overalls and a white t-shirt. He was so big he didn't get up a lot, just sat in his recliner. One day a squirrel chewed its way through the soffit of his house and got inside. The next time we visited Grandpa Cramer, he had made that squirrel his pet, and it would sleep on his chest just underneath his bibs. He'd be leaning back in his big recliner as the squirrel's tail would stick out the top of his overalls and tickle his chin. It was weird but we convinced him we thought it was cool.

Getting back to dip bait, Grandpa Cramer would drive to some cheese factory in Wisconsin and harvest a waste byproduct of the cheese-making process for part of his magical concoction. He'd add a bunch of other ingredients and let it sit in the sun and ripen. I only have a half a dozen regrets in life so far. One of those regrets my brother and I share is not getting Grandpa Cramer's dip bait recipe before he passed away.

I don't know if he was a squirrel whisperer, but I do know he was a catfish whisperer. His dip bait was guaranteed to catch catfish. We'd use a stick and push a rubber worm with deep ribbing and a treble hook to the bottom of the jar of brown goo, trying not to get any on our fingers. Then, using a combination of an egg weight and small twig tied to the line just a foot above the bait, we'd cast the rig out to the deepest part of the lake we could reach with our old Zebco33. We'd prop the pole on the bank with a "Y" shaped branch stuck in the mud and clip a little brass bell to the tip of the pole. When the catfish would grab the bait and run with it, the bell would ring and we knew landing the fish was the only thing that stood between us and dinner.

On this particular trip, against our recommendation, my dad brought a can of baked beans. My brother and I looked at each other in disgust. It wasn't his lack of confidence in our fishing abilities that offended us--it was the fact my brother and I hated baked beans.

I almost had to pick a different best friend as a kid because of baked beans. I loved hanging out with my friend Isaac. We loved baseball, Star Wars, and building forts in our back yards. But when I would go to his house, they always had baked beans for lunch.

Everyday! I'm not kidding. Every time. And their house smelled funny. I was sure there was a correlation. Sometimes his mom would cut up a hot dog and throw it in the pot and so I'd pick out the pieces of hot dog. Chunks of hot dog literally saved my friendship with Isaac.

Despite our assurances we didn't need a can of beans, my dad threw it in the pack anyway.

Now, when we get to heaven someday and if they play the video of this event, it may be different than what I'm about to describe. If you were to ask my Dad and my brother, the details of this memory may be different for them, but here is how I recall it.

After dad got off work on a Friday, we took our little V-bottom boat loaded with all of our supplies, and the three of us puttered our way across the lake to a little island in the middle. We set up our tent and a little makeshift kitchen complete with one of those classic green Coleman stoves with double burners. This was where we would fry up all the fish we would catch. Then we rigged up all of our fishing poles with egg weights and ridge worms, and then covered them in Grandpa Cramer's magic dip bait. We cast them all in different directions as far as little Zebco33 reels would allow. After we'd propped them with sticks on the bank, we attached the bells and waited for dinner.

Darkness came. No fish. But dad assured us that the best catfishing happens at night, and so we lit the lantern and kept fishing through the night, reeling in every fifteen minutes to apply a fresh coating of dip bait. At ten p.m., hunger pains started to remind us of our failure as fishermen. The lack of nutrition must have started impacting my brain, and so after checking and re-dipping the bait, I forgot to remove the bell before I cast. Into the night, three splashes. The weight, the bait and the bell. We all knew right away what I'd done. I felt terrible.

We crawled into the tent that night certain we would be awakened by the sound of one of those bells, only to have the sun come up. No fish. We checked our poles. Nothing but clean ridge worms.

No breakfast. We kept fishing.

No lunch, but we kept fishing.

I had never in my short life experienced this kind of hunger. It felt like my stomach was eating itself. Around dinnertime my dad reached for that can of beans, and I'm pretty sure I saw tears in my little brother's eyes.

Dad cooked that can of beans over that old green Coleman camp stove. Then he led us in a prayer thanking God for baked beans and asking Him to provide some fish. And for the first time in my life, I realized how much I love baked beans. So delicious. They were amazing. With the nutrients and protein now feeding our brains, we decided to do something different. Instead of casting as far as we could, we didn't cast at all. We pushed the button on our little bullet reels, releasing the line right next to the shore.

We fished through the night, finally tucking ourselves into our sleeping bags long after dark. And then, in the middle of the night, I learned what an answered prayer sounds like.

To a couple of little boys from Illinois, the provision of God sounds like a catfish bell interrupting the rhythmic serenade of crickets in the middle of the night. We bolted out of that sleeping bag, and we lit the lantern as dad started to reel in the fish. It was a fighter! My brother and I were anxious. We watched the tip of the pole arc toward the water as my dad leaned back unable to disguise his own excitement. "Please Lord, help me land this fish!" he prayed out loud. "Yes Lord!" my brother and I chimed in.

Finally, dad lifted the pole and onto the bank slid the prized provision. Flopping ferociously, revealed by the golden flame of our lantern was a two-pound catfish. Dad fired up that stove and got the frying pan warmed up. We watched as he cleaned the catfish and then cut the meaty fillets into chunks. He pulled a half stick of butter and a Ziploc baggy of flour out of the cooler. A few moments later my brother and I learned what the provision of God tastes like. I've eaten a lot of great meals in my lifetime but few are as memorable as those flaky hot chunks of catfish fried in a skillet on a little island in the middle of the night.

Even now as a grown man the lesson is not lost. God promises to provide for all of our needs. I keep a catfish bell clipped to my rearview mirror even today, so I'll never forget the time God provided catfish for two hungry little boys. Seeing the bell everyday reminds me that no matter what I need, God loves to break the silence of my waiting with the ringing bell of His provision.

TAKEAWAY:

Take 90 seconds and thank God for all the places He's provided in your past. Where are the areas in your life you're currently waiting for God's provision?

10

• • •

Kayak Envy

"So if we have enough food and clothing, let us be content."[11] – *The Apostle Paul, 1 Timothy 6:6*

We usually spend under a hundred bucks for a child's birthday in our house. However, the summer my oldest son celebrated his fifteenth birthday, I wanted to do something special. We decided to get him a kayak so we could spend some time on the Spoon River together. I knew a kayak was going to be a stretch for us financially, more than double what we had budgeted. Having chosen to have seven kids and be a one-income family, I understand I have forfeited any rights to complain about our financial situation.

Later that summer I planned a special day for my son and me to go kayaking. First, I was going to get some work done around the farm. Then, we were going to take those kayaks out to the lake. Plus there was a generous family that had just bought a house on this lake. The house came with bunk beds, and they were giving us three sets of bunk beds. Since my wife's sister and her family were in town from Pennsylvania, we could load up the bunk beds, hang out at the lake with the in-laws, and then I could get some kayak time with my son. It was going to be great day.

But my day was derailed. As I'm up next to the barn at the other end of our property, I see my brother-in-law pull into our driveway in his new Suburban. It's a nice Suburban. But he doesn't just pull in. He backs in. With a trailer full of really sharp looking Sea-Doos. Black and white with gold pinstripes. He jumps out and I hear him holler at my wife and kids, "Who wants to go to the river today?!" My heart sinks. I start to walk up to the house while they're loading up, and my wife says, "Aren't you going to join us?" "No honey, I told this family I would pick up the bunk beds before two o'clock. I can't." A few minutes later I wave goodbye to my family as they head in the opposite direction for the day.

"Scott, you are such a loser," I think to myself. "You busted the bank on a $225 kayak. You'll never be able to compete for your kid's attention against a guy with better toys."

After I pull out of the driveway in my '77 Ford pickup, I have a mini midlife crisis. I begin to wrestle with the question, "Am I making enough money for my family or have I sacrificed the best wage-earning years of my life to ministry?"

As they are headed to the river, I'm feeling insecure in my ability to provide for my family. When I get to the couple's new house to get the bunk beds, I see their brand-new Silverado hooked up to aluminum car hauler. It was a sweet rig. The husband points to his truck and trailer and says, "Scott, you should just borrow this to get these bunk beds to your house."

I look at my '77 Ford pick-up with rickety old trailer and notice the wheel-wells are considerably rustier than I had remembered. Then I look at his rig. Their daughter is back from college and she's in the cab using the truck's Wi-Fi to order Chicago Cub's tickets for tomorrow's game.

I am having trouble being content.

We start to load the bunk beds onto his trailer, and I notice how nice these bunk beds are. Nicer than anything I could afford on my single income. I had grown up sleeping in bunk beds that had evenly spaced two by fours with plywood panels supporting the mattress. These bunk beds came with mini box springs! And the mattresses... wow. Quality must equate to heavy. These would be best mattresses in our house. Such a generous couple.

We finally get everything loaded and as I'm headed down the road, I look in the rearview mirror only to see one of the top mattresses start to flap. I slow down, but it doesn't help. Vwoosh! The mattress on one of the top bunks goes flying up into the air. Now it's lying in the middle of Knox County Highway 12. What do you do? I'm not going to back the trailer up on the highway. I pull over and throw the hazards on. I get out and walk back to the mattress. It must have been a quarter mile.

Returning to my truck, I'm now walking down the highway with a mattress over my head as cars are zipping by. Did I mention the better the quality of mattress the heavier it is? By this time pictures of my family enjoying themselves on the river are starting to pop up on my brother-in-law's social media.

I get back to the truck and throw the mattress on the lower bunk. I look at what is now the box spring alone on the top bunk of one of the beds and think, "That box spring is heavy enough. I'll go slowly."

I'm going nice and slow with my hazards on, and after a few minutes I look in the rearview mirror and notice the box spring is gone. I didn't even see it fly off. So I pull over again, put on the hazards, and walk the ditches back a mile or more on each side.

Weeds up to my waist.

Nothing.

I can't find it.

I get back in that truck and I say something out loud that shocks me when I hear it leave my lips. I said, "Scott, you don't deserve nice stuff." I remember those words caused me to flinch.

I got home and I realized not only did I have a contentment

problem, but I felt the danger of speaking a curse over my life. I could sense I was taking myself out of position for God's blessing.

And then, I asked God for help, "Lord, what am I doing?" I didn't hear an audible voice, but I certainly felt like God dropped a word in my heart that day. I wrote this down on a sticky note and put it somewhere I could be reminded of it every day. I felt like God said, "Why not treat what you've got like it's a lot? Even if it's not."

Later that evening my brother-in-law and I were sitting on my front porch. He said, "You ok? Seems like something's wrong." I wanted to scream, "Yes something's wrong! My family just got hijacked by a guy with cooler stuff! And you're my brother-in-law so I still have to be nice to you!"

In a moment of transparency, I was able to be honest with him. He said something to help me put everything in perspective. "The greatest enemy of contentment is comparison." He began to tell me what he saw, simply describing the way God had blessed me, my family, our ministry, and how I now had nicer bunk beds than he did.

Envy had blinded me to all God had blessed me with. Something changed when I started to "treat what I got like it's a lot." My gratitude increased. I became more thankful.

If you treat what you've got like it's a lot, you can't help but be thankful for it.

TAKEAWAY:

Where has envy blinded you?

Why do we constantly think we're missing something?

11

• • •

Ripped Pants

"Above all else, guard your heart, for everything you do flows from it."
                          - *King Solomon, Proverbs 4:23 (NIV)*

I was a good Baptist kid growing up. Which means I was really well behaved, on Sundays. I remember attending a little Baptist church as early as four years old. I remember flannel graph storyboards during Sunday school. I remember "kite Sundays" in the spring when everyone who attended got an old-fashioned paper kite. My brother and I would take the wooden sticks and string and make a bow and arrow.

I still remember my favorite Sunday school teacher, Mrs. Willard. She gave us candy if we could recite a verse. I remember "Old-Fashioned Sunday" when everyone dressed up like they were from the 1800's. I loved that Sunday because it was the only Sunday I could wear blue jeans. I'd go barefoot with a rope belt and tell people I was Huck Finn. I'm so thankful for the heritage of faith I received in that little Baptist church as a kid and on into my young adult years.

We had a small youth group at this church, which included all of the kids from junior high and high school. We would play ping pong and foosball. My youth pastor yelled at me once because I played a Beach Boys cassette on the big stereo cabinet. The house of God was no place for the devil's music. I stopped listening to The Beach Boys…in church.

Once a year our youth group would take over the adult services. We called it "Youth Sunday," and it filled the place as parents would come just to support their kids' participation in the service.

One of the girls would play the prelude and postlude on the piano. Never a guitar or drums. Those were the devil's instruments. On rare occasion an instrumental cassette tape could be used for a special number. But this was risky. The cassette tape couldn't include guitar or drums. Usually, a couple of the girls would sing a duet.

Most of the times I can remember they ended up giggling uncontrollably, making it impossible for them to finish. The guys were just ushers. They would receive the offering and hand out bulletins. Usually the oldest guy in the youth group at the time would give a short little devotional, and the second oldest guy in the group would do announcements just before the youth pastor would bring the message.

I was thirteen when I had the job of announcements. This also happened to be the year of my biggest growth spurt. I grew eight inches that year. I remember finding these red horizontal lines on my waistline around my back. I asked my mom what they were. "Stretch marks," my mom said. My knees hurt all the time. The doctors had me wearing these special shoe inserts and said, "Those are growing pains because you're growing so fast."

With the exception of "Old-Fashioned Sunday," everyone got dressed up at this church. I'd wear slacks, a collared shirt, occasionally a tie--and there might have been a sweater vest or two in there. But I didn't have a great selection. I got a new outfit for Easter and another for Christmas. I made a combination of last year's Easter outfit and the clothes from Christmas past work throughout the year.

Needless to say my clothes didn't keep up with my growth spurt the particular year I had been assigned the announcements for Youth Sunday. This year my pants were tight. Too tight.

During rehearsal, about an hour before people would start arriving, we were practicing our parts. As I'm walking up the stairs to the stage, my pants decide they had fought the battle long enough. I heard fabric rip just behind me, and I felt a new relaxed comfort in my pants that I hadn't felt in long time.

Somehow standing behind the big Baptist pulpit, I managed to get through my part at rehearsal, and as soon as I was done, I went to the bathroom to try to assess the damage in the mirror. But I couldn't get turned around far enough to see it. I could feel the hole in my pants, but I couldn't tell if it was something that could be seen.

When service starts, I'm absolutely distracted and worried about the hole in the seat of my pants. The moment arrives when the last song ends, and I must now walk up those eight giant steps to the stage with my backside exposed to the sanctuary full of people. I stood behind the big pulpit and looked at a sanctuary full of people. I see my best friend Jeremy smiling and laughing slightly as he pretends to pick his nose.

I choked.

I just completely forgot what I was supposed to say. I thought I'd memorized it so I didn't have any notes. I remember looking at all those people and being so distracted by the fact they may have seen my underwear, and I was sure my friend was snickering for this reason.

I must have managed to mumble my way through something because I remember exactly what it looks like for an audience to feel sorry for the speaker. Oh, the looks on their faces said it so clearly. I'd blown it. Eventually I went and sat down. It was the most embarrassing moment of my life up until that point.

While my pants lost a battle of the bulge, the enemy won a very different battle. It was the battle for my heart. When I left church that day, I made a promise to myself that I would never speak in front of a group of people again. Little did I know twenty-five years later, I would work for a church where one of my primary Sunday responsibilities as a campus pastor would be, can you guess? Yep. Announcements.

And then I realized this: Satan doesn't fight fair. He doesn't wait for you to grow up and become mature. He'll find a time when you're weak or tired. He'll look for an opportunity when you're hungry, alone or embarrassed, and he'll attack you in the very place where God has plans to use you to make the greatest impact in this world.

So, in the words of the wisest person in history, found in Proverbs 4:23, "Guard your heart above all else, for it determines the course of your life."

TAKEAWAY:

Is there a place of past failure or embarrassment where you have unknowingly made a vow?

What if the enemy's greatest battle for your heart is an indication of where God wants to use you?

Part Three

• • •

And then...Love

12

• • •

Peter's Casting Call

"Lord, should we fight? We brought the swords!" [12]
— *Peter, Luke 22:49-50*

Of all the disciples, Peter is my favorite. I think this is true for all of us. We can relate to him at some point in our journey.

When I was in college, I attended a church where we did an Easter musical. This little passion play was our outreach to our community each year. The role of Jesus was always reserved for a few special members of our church who could pull it off. Usually it went back and forth between a former pastor and a guy who actually possessed acting experience. You didn't ask to be Jesus. You were approached by the director, and she would ask you to be Jesus.

But the rest of us regular guys didn't really want to take our shirt off and hang on a cross in front of the entire community. We just wanted to be a soldier or a disciple or something with a little less pressure to perform. And if we were a disciple, we wanted to be Peter. The role of Peter came with some freedom. Freedom to be gruff. Deep down we knew this role wasn't really a very far stretch from reality. Playing Peter was easy. He was passionate, immature, misunderstood, fickle, angry--he probably smelled funny. And when he spoke, I'm noticing throughout scripture more frequently than not, it was followed by a reprimand from a carpenter.

But something happens to Peter in the Garden of Gethsemane. I mean, look, Peter is passionate. He says this at dinner just before they head to the Garden: "...I will never fall away...Even if I must die with you, I will never deny you."[13] After the Garden, he's hiding, denying Christ: "I do not know the man."[14]

The rooster crows.[15]

What happened in the Garden within the span of about thirty-five verses?

Have you ever wondered why Peter cut off the guard's ear? Because he missed his neck! I'm convinced Peter was trying to cut off the man's head! This wasn't Peter trying to be Zorro. He was carrying a gladiator sword!

Peter, whom Jesus chose to be a fisher of men. This Peter spent three years with Jesus. He listened to Jesus teach, saw miracles, walked on water. This same Peter witnessed God in the Flesh healing, feeding, teaching, and loving people. This Peter on whom Jesus was going to build his church, was packing heat in today's terms. He's got his concealed carry card for his sword. And he draws first blood!

If Jesus came to start a revolution the way Peter thought in this moment in the Garden, I think Peter would have fought to the death for Jesus. "Even if I must die with you, I will not deny you!" he said.

Instead, there is a turning point. Here is where things shifted from dedication to denial. Jesus rocked Peter's world when he picked up the man's ear and reattached it to the very head Peter was trying to split.

Peter witnesses Jesus loving his enemy the way Jesus loves Peter.

That must have blown his mind. Think about it. This is the moment Peter was ready for. Let's fight! Jesus' response to Peter's boldness and passion sends him reeling into the confusion we witness in just the next thirty-five verses of the same chapter... "I don't know the man," Peter denied. I think Peter was telling the truth. This is not how Peter saw Jesus going out.[16]

If you spent a day with Jesus, how many ears would he need to reattach in the wake of your "passion"?

And then, I realized this: if I could spend a day with Jesus, I wonder how many ears he would have to reattach in the aftermath of my vision of how I think His kingdom should look here on Earth. I wonder how many ears I have slashed in the path of my "leadership" and my "discipleship."

More than I know.

I've taken my swings with this sword.

TAKEAWAY

Who are some of the people in your life that have suffered at the expense of your passionate "sword swinging"?

What could you do today to help them look to Jesus as the one who reattaches ears?

13

• • •

Help Me Love You

"Love your neighbor as yourself." – Jesus, Matthew 22:36-39

Why is this command so hard? Don't judge me--you know it's hard too. Their music is too loud. Their friends park on your grass. It's hard sometimes to love the people in my house, let alone the people who live in my neighborhood.

It's so easy to gloss over this verse. I begin to believe, "I can see why Jesus loves me. I can even make the argument why He would die for me, but for Billy? Wow. (Sigh) God must really love people." I've never said that out loud. But I've thought it.

I might even be struggling with an individual and I'll pray, "Lord, help me to see Bob the way You see him." Or "Heavenly Father, give me your eyes. Help me see this neighborhood the way You do. God help me to see my coworker, family member, ex-spouse, fill in the blank, the way You see them."

Sounds like a noble prayer. Right?

It's not.

It wasn't until my wife and I were having dinner with some other adoptive families that God gave me the revelation I didn't know I needed. We were sitting in the host couple's living room, the kids were all playing upstairs, and the conversation turned into a little support group discussing some of the challenges associated with adoption. Joyce, one of moms, said, "Sometimes I just pray, 'God help me to see Samantha the way you see….'" And in my mind, I was way ahead of her. In my mind I was already thinking "Preach it sister! Help me see Hana the way you see Hana. God, help Joyce to see Samantha the way you see Samantha." But she didn't say that.

What she said rocked my world. She said, "God help me see Samantha the way that you see…me."

It took my breath away. Literally. I heard myself gasp a little. I looked around at the other couples. Where they as shocked by that revelation? Did they hear me gasp? Or did they already get it? I was the token pastor in the room. I was supposed to already get it. I was too embarrassed to say, "Whoa, whoa, wait…what?! What did you just say? Can we just land there for a second?"

And then, God exposed my pride and he broke my heart… again. Hana is our daughter from Ethiopia. We knew there would be possible developmental challenges with Hana when we adopted her. But add to it the more common issues with orphans like Reactive Attachment Disorder and you have a recipe for a better prayer life.

"God, help me to see Hana the way that you see me."

When we forget, no, when I forget, that I am desperate for God's grace, I am blinded from seeing and loving others the way Jesus loves me.

Pastor, author and speaker Mark Batterson says it this way, "Our biggest failures are our failures to extend the same grace to others that God has extended to us."[17]

Today, I couldn't tell you if Hana really is a beautiful young lady who loves animals and shows love to others by serving them… or if God is just helping me see her the way He sees me. Either way, I'll take it.

Things have changed.

I wonder what the world would look like if everyone who said they followed Jesus, the 2.2 billion people in the world who claim to be a Christian, extended the same grace they've received. What if Christ followers everywhere began to love others the way that God has loved them?

Whoa, that might just change the world.

TAKEAWAY

Who do you need to love the way God loves you?

How can you do that today?

14

• • •

Tie Some Shoes

"Don't be selfish; don't try to impress others. Be humble,
thinking of others as better than yourselves."
-The Apostle Paul, Philippians 2:3-5

We were looking to add an associate pastor to our staff when I was the head of one of the Multisite campuses at our church. I put together the job description, including normal things like help cover pastoral care responsibilities – weddings, funerals, baptisms, child dedications, coaching/mentoring, hospital and nursing home visits, teaching and leading. Typical responsibilities someone looking to fill this role would expect. But at the last minute as I was making the final decision to hire one of my good friends in ministry, I added a line, "wipe down urinals between services, clean up puke, and generally 'wash others' feet'."

I thought I was so clever. These were things I had done but I thought, "I'm such an innovative, creative boss. Teaching my team how to be servants. I'm such a humble leader." When you acknowledge your own humility, that's pride. It's a complex cycle. If you think you're humble, you're not.

James 4:6 says, "God opposes the proud but shows favor to the humble." (NIV)[18] And that's what happened. God decided to exercise His sense of humor. I submitted the official job description, our new associate pastor accepted, and on his first Sunday I noticed he was in containment mode with a one of our guests in the lobby. At the end of the day, as a Multisite campus pastor, if we do nothing else, our ultimate responsibility on a Sunday is to create a safe and distraction-free environment for guests to worship, learn about and ultimately meet Jesus. This occasionally means giving a little extra attention to certain guests. This guest was drunk. And loud. We didn't know his name but he insisted we call him "Uncle Rooster." He didn't tell us why. But here I am sitting at ten minutes until the second service dismisses and third service guests begin to arrive, and I'm smelling alcohol and a potential conflict. So, as lovingly as I can, I convince this man that it's a good idea to watch the message in our lobby and then not to linger too long. All of a sudden he looks at me and his eyes get big as bloodshot cue balls and he says, "I gotta go to da bafroom." Yes he talked like Scooby-Doo. Drunk Scooby.

This guy can't even walk in a straight line. So I go in with him. I'm watching the clock, and I've got three minutes to isolate this situation away from the crowd. I'm waiting for him as he's standing at the urinal, and I notice there is some water spilled on the counter top. I rip off a couple of paper towels from the dispenser and wipe the countertops down. There are water spots on the mirror. I make a circular motion with the paper towel until the spots disappear. Then I notice there are some pieces of paper on the floor and I pick those up and throw them in the garbage. I just want everything to look nice as new guests come in. This bathroom is sparkling.

Then I hear water running. I look back to the counter top to see if I bumped a faucet and accidentally left it on. Nothing. I look back towards the urinals and stalls and realize it's not water I hear.

Uncle Rooster is standing directly in front of the urinal but he isn't hitting the target. Pee is going everywhere! All over the floor and his shoes--but he doesn't know it. He's babbling on and on in his drunk Scooby voice about how I'm his "beft and only fwend" and he "wuvs dis church so much." I'm only thinking one thing, "as soon as he steps out of the way, I've got to get this cleaned up! I've got less than a minute before service ends, and this bathroom gets packed with people." Usually I would grab some rubber gloves before I cleaned up something like this, but there was no time. I wrap both hands in paper towels until they look like big white boxing gloves. He finally finishes and steps out of the way and I hit the floor to start cleaning. I'm Danielson training under Mr. Miyagi's instruction. Wax on, wax off. I'm on all fours wiping up this floor and he's still rambling. Suddenly he plops his urine-soaked foot right under my nose and says, "Can you tie my shoe?"

I remember the job description I recently edited and think, "Where is the new associate pastor?!" This would be a great lesson in humility for him. But apparently it was me that needed the lesson. And then, I remember, God opposes the proud. I remember having this thought, "Jesus would tie this man's shoe."

So, with my face less than two feet from this man's wet and smelly shoe laces I said, "Yes. Yes, I can." And I did.

Looking back, it wasn't so much a lesson in humility. It was about simply loving another human being. A human being made in the image of God.

Maybe, for a moment, Uncle Rooster felt loved enough to begin to believe that the best version of himself was still in the future. Or maybe God knew someone who needed to see their pastor in that position. Whatever the reason, I hope you're never asked to tie someone's urine-soaked shoelaces. But I'm certain there will be another way God will ask you to "be humble and think of others as better than yourselves."

TAKEAWAY

What are some ways you can "tie some shoes"?

Commit now to being ready and willing for the opportunities to be like Jesus to those whom with you come in contact today.

15

• • •

Greater Love

"Greater love has no one than this: to lay down one's life for one's friends."[19] *– Jesus, John 15:3*

How long could you love someone if they never loved you back? Most of you, like me, would probably agree that if we express love, or kindness, or generosity and it's not reciprocated in a certain amount of time, we're moving on. Whether it's a neighbor or a co-worker or even a family member, I'm only going to invest so much energy and emotion before I need to see a payback.

Sounds incredibly selfish when I read these words, but just think about the relationships in your life. It's true. I mean, we expect a thank you card, an invite reciprocated, a hug, a look or a smile. We need some symbol or signal that gives us the feeling of appreciation. A favor returned, a text or a shout out on social media. Anything. But it's got to come back or if enough time goes by without those things, we're out.

Reciprocation.

In life, in relationships, adoption, leadership and ministry...it doesn't always happen that way.

I remember talking to my good friend right before his oldest son was headed off to college. They were a close family and his relationship with his oldest son was as solid as any I had witnessed. I was envious. They had become more than father and son. By his own admission they'd become good friends. They shared a deep love for each other. But here is the funny thing about this relationship as college approached. The father was deeply saddened by the thought of his future without his son, while the son never had more hope or happiness for his future...without his father.

Things will never be the same. Two people in a relationship who meet a season of separation with two inverse outlooks on their future.

I used to work in our family's glass business, and I remember fixing a window in the attic of an old two-story Victorian house. I saw this old Norman Rockwell painting leaning against the base of a wall there. The painting depicted a father and son sitting on the tailgate of a pickup truck waiting for the train. The father, his head hung low, cigarette barely hanging from his lips. His posture slumped and his clothes clean but worked in and well worn. His hair disheveled. The son, however, is in his suit with perfect posture sitting up straight. He's got a new haircut, a smile on his face, suitcase at his feet. The "State" sticker stuck to the suitcase made it obvious they were waiting for the train that would take the boy to the big university. The father was looking one direction past his son, and the son was looking the other way, his eyes are fixed far down... the future. Even the dog in the picture knew something was worth grieving in this moment.

When a father hurts alone, that's hard. When a father's hurt is met with a son's hope, that's harder. This kind of love won't be coming back. At least not for another four years or so.

I'll never forget the lesson our daughter from Ethiopia taught us about this kind of love. The first several years after adopting her were full of opportunities to love without reciprocation. Here is what we learned: love is easy…when it's reciprocated. But until you experience a prolonged drought that requires so much emotional equity up front, every day, you really don't know how hard love can be.

With our biological kids during that season, my love always came back, eventually. Even now, after a difficult day, I'll get it back. It might come at story time when they put their head on my shoulder. It might be a simple smile and a wink at just the right time. Sometimes it's a "thank you" card for a daddy daughter date night. When my son Evan was three, he would tell me I was his "best daddy" right before he would fall asleep. You see? I got it back. It's not much, but at the same time it's more than enough.

And then, those years after our adoption, I learned when we love there is no guarantee that it will come back or be appreciated. That's why love needs to be unconditional. We would love and love and love her, only to be pushed away.

What our new daughter was showing me and the way she was making me feel, is how God must feel. A lot. God loves and loves and pursues us. God desires a relationship with us. That's why we were originally created. Adam and Eve, and God, walking in the garden. And now we push Him away.

God never stops loving us. He never changes. "But God showed his great love for us by sending Christ to die for us while we were still sinners."[20] Wow. Greater love.

I thought I was a pretty nice guy. A loving guy. But I'm finding out, I'm pretty selfish. And I'm finding out that this unconditional love is a greater love. But it's easier to talk about on Sunday than to practice on Monday. I'm not even sure if I fully understand this kind of love because deep down inside of my current situation, I'm still hopeful. For what? That I'll get it back.

Like the fathers mentioned before, the sons will return. With a fiancé, new stories, new dreams and sometimes… new debt. More to love.

But for now, God is giving me a glimpse of His love for me.

And it's a challenge. Perhaps that is why, "Greater love has no one than this: to lay down one's life for one's friend."[21] Maybe giving up your life is the greatest love because at that point, there is no future chance for reciprocation. It's given.

Then it's over.

I may never fully understand or truly demonstrate this kind of love on this side of eternity. But, oh what difference it would make in every relationship. At work, in our marriage, with our neighbors or our kids.

This love…is a "Greater Love."

TAKEAWAY:

What are some tangible ways we can allow this "greater love" to infiltrate our relationships today?

Part Four

. . .

And then...ADVENTURE

16

• • •

Just You

"One thing you lack, go sell everything you have and give to the poor, and you will have treasure in heaven. Then come, follow me." [22] *– Jesus, Mark 10:17-22*

When I was twenty years old, my brother and I borrowed $3,000 from my dad. Dad charged us 7 percent interest annually on any unpaid balance. I include this detail for my kids who have borrowed money from me…interest free. My brother and I used the borrowed money to purchase a used "Sno-Shak." We wanted to try our hand at selling shaved ice at Galesburg's Railroad Days. The Sno-Shak was a baby blue concession trailer shaped like a hut with hardened spray foam on the roof painted white to look like snow. The front roof fascia was lined with bug light bulbs that would give off a yellow hue at night.

It was awesome.

We had stumbled across the sugary, shaved ice concoction while on a job site for our glass business in a neighboring community. The Sno-shak was just big enough for two people inside. My brother and

I would take turns. One of us would shave a block of ice into the cups as fast as we could. We shoved a block of ice into the machine and then tapped on the sewing machine style pedal with our foot. This would push the block of ice into the three razor sharp blades, shooting the perfect texture of snow ice into a Styrofoam cup. The other brother would take the order, take the money, and pour the sugary-flavored syrup of choice into the ice.

We had the system down. Cost of goods sold per cup was twenty-eight cents. We were charging two dollars for the medium and one dollar more for the large. We even reduced our flavor choices down to four instead of the normal eighteen because we knew kids would just stare at the menu while others waited. We wanted to sell as many snow cones as possible in the least amount of time.

We moved the Sno-Shak into position with the other street vendors at six a.m. on Saturday morning. We wouldn't stop working until ten p.m., and then do it again Sunday until three p.m. It was a blast. It was delicious. It was exhausting. On a hot weekend with a three on three tournament, we would be non-stop busy. Literally no break for lunch or dinner, just taking care of the next person in line.

I remember the first year on the Saturday night when we finally closed and turned off the yellow bug lights on the front of the shack. We started to clean up and count our money. We didn't have a cash register. We just had this metal box that didn't even lock. It was packed full of bills. There was over $1,500 in cash that night! This was the first time my brother and I had seen that kind of money.

Have you ever seen what $1,500 in dollar bills looks like? It looked like a million bucks to us! I remember thinking, "I wonder if this is what it feels like to be rich?"

I can still see it in my mind. The carnival was still going on downtown so there were lights, noise, people, and a concert at the beer tent. We were the last vendors there of the "funnel-cake" and "lemonade shake-up" variety, if you know what I mean. Now we needed to walk about three blocks to our vehicle in the dark past a lot of people. You know, the kind of people who are still at a carnival after ten p.m. You can imagine the kind. Not sober, not safe.

I took that wad of cash and stuffed it in the front pocket of my shorts. It barely fit.

Then I headed out, afraid. I thought to myself, "Maybe 'this' is what it feels like to be rich." Afraid. Afraid of all I have and to lose it.

Just so you know, after we paid my dad back the loan and added up all the supply costs, we had each made a total of three hundred bucks that weekend. Not bad. But not rich. But perhaps for a few minutes of my life, I knew what it felt like to be rich. If so, then it feels like this; work sun up to sun down, make a lot of money and then worry about someone else taking it.

I've never been rich. Really, I haven't. My family has had some good years and some tough years. Nevertheless, most of the time growing up in the family business and pursing a journey called ministry, we just thanked God for His provision.

I know what it's like to try to survive seventh grade wearing generic shoes. I know what it's like to check out at the grocery store with a cart full of white and yellow packages with black letters. It's much cooler to buy generic today. The packaging doesn't give you away.

I'll bet most of you reading this are like me. No matter what the reality of our circumstances growing up, you may or may not remember growing up poor, but you do remember...not being rich. Am I right? We don't remember being poor. But most of us would say, "I do remember... NOT being rich."

Jesus had some tough words for a rich young ruler one day. His conversation is recorded in scripture. He said, "Go, and sell all your possessions, and give the money to the poor, and you will have treasure in heaven; then come, follow me."[22]

If you're like me, you've probably blown by this passage many times with little conviction.

Knowing that I've never been rich and you've probably never

been rich, we should be able to read this quickly and say to ourselves, "Yep, got it. No need to camp here long. What else you got Jesus?"

But I can't. This passage challenges me. Jesus says many things that challenge me.

Things like, "So those who are last now will be first then, and those who are first will be last.[23] Or how about the fact that it's easier to live off of ninety percent of our income rather than one hundred percent? As someone with a degree in economics, that one still amazes me. But this passage in the Gospel of Mark might take the cake.

For starters, we know that Jesus has compassion for the outcasts, prostitutes and others. [24] Jesus was a friend of "tax collectors and sinners…" In fact, he makes one of them (Matthew) a disciple. Jesus was accused of being a glutton and a drunkard because of the crowd he would hang out with.[25] He even tells a stinky, foul-mouthed fisherman (Peter), "You will be the rock on which the church will be built."[26]

And there is this guy. The rich young ruler. He is well dressed and clean cut. He's a wise young man who has worked hard and invested well. He's kept all the commandments and made good financial decisions. The whole Bible is full of God's heart, which reflects a relentless pursuit of people. It doesn't make sense for Jesus to turn this guy away. But Jesus does. Because he's rich?! What?!

I'd have made him the chairman of my elder board. I'd have picked this guy for my all-star ministry team. I'd have made him CFO of my organization. The chairman of the board for my nonprofit. I'd have put this guy on a box of "Wheaties"! Jesus didn't. In essence, He says get rid of everything until all you have is you. Just bring you "and then…" we'll go.

"Teacher, what must I do to inherit eternal life?" Funny how the answer is standing right in front of him.

Mark 10:21 says, "Jesus looked at him and loved him…." I love the fact that Mark, the author of this passage, knew Jesus well

And Then . . .

enough to recognize something about Christ's posture, or his facial expression or the tone of his voice, to indicate Jesus loved him. This is refreshingly hopeful to me.

And then, Jesus said, "…You lack one thing. Go, sell all that you have and give to the poor, and you will have treasure in heaven; and come, follow me."

Do you see it? Jesus says, "You lack one thing," but then he gives him three things to do!

Sell everything.

Give to the poor.

Follow me.

Jesus says, "One thing you lack, do these three things."

I think the "one thing" is the last thing, but Jesus knew the man couldn't get there without the first two.

Jesus is saying, "You" follow me. Just "you." Not your stuff. Not your worry. Not your management abilities. Not your skills. Jesus just wants all of "you."

I want eternal life too. But do I want Jesus?

I want God to keep my children safe. But do I want them to follow Jesus…into the mission field?

We want God to grow our business and our church. But do we want Jesus?

We want to spend eternity in heaven. But do we want to spend it with Jesus?

Like the rich man, the answer stands in front of us.

What if God called you to a life of obscurity? No social media followers. No stage. No books to write. Just following and being obedient to him. Is Jesus enough?

Maybe you're not rich. Maybe you think you have nothing to give. Not talented. Not educated. Not wealthy, witty or wise. What if you're closer to being used by God than you think? Maybe if we had those "riches" He'd ask us to lay them down anyway.

He wants just you, "And then…" He says, "Follow me."

TAKEAWAY:

What are the "riches" in your life that are keeping you from following Jesus?

17

• • •

Jesus Died for Jerks

"My Father! If it is possible, let this cup of suffering be taken away from me. Yet I want your will to be done, not mine." - Jesus in the Garden of Gethsemane, Matthew 26:39

When my wife and I were in Israel recently, our group paid a visit to the Garden of Gethsemane. I mean we literally paid a visit. We had to pay four shekels to some guy at the front gate in order to get in. The Garden of Gethsemane is the place where Jesus prayed this right before he was to be arrested and later crucified, "My Father! If it is possible, let this cup of suffering be taken away from me. Yet I want your will to be done, not mine."

It's the place where Jesus sweat blood.

Where Jesus asked his disciples to pray, but they fell asleep.

Where Jesus was betrayed with a kiss.

Where Peter drew his sword.

Where Jesus reattached an ear.

I was standing in this very place just below the Mount of Olives.

I scooped up a handful of dirt and put it in my backpack, which I'm not sure is legal. But like a soldier on foreign soil, I wanted some reminder of having been here.

We walked into the Garden area, gated and surrounded by a stone wall, ten foot tall. Visiting Israel is an all-out information overload on your brain and energy. It is non-stop from one significant location to another. However, this was one of the few times during the trip where we were encouraged to find the shade of an olive tree and just sit. Quietly. Reflecting, praying, reading.

It was during this time I opened my Bible and read Matthew chapter twenty-six. As I read I was struck with this thought. This is the moment Jesus could have backed out. This is the moment you or I would have backed out. I know I would have.

As I sit quietly under an olive tree, I listen to the sounds of the old city. I hear traffic just outside the walls, honking horns and engines revving. I can hear the street vendors yelling in languages I couldn't understand, selling their souvenirs to tourists like me. I hear the "tink tink" of shekels being dropped in the jar at the front gate. I can hear an annoying pastor from another church speaking loudly to his group just behind us on the upper terrace.

I'm trying to concentrate on this passage in scripture, this moment in Biblical history. I'm trying to reflect on Jesus' sacrifice, and I'm desperate for a quiet moment with God to hear from Him in this sacred place. Instead, I find myself getting frustrated with the distractions. "What a bunch of jerks," I think to myself. "Doesn't this other pastor know that there are other groups here? Moreover, shouldn't the people who live in this land understand the sacred nature of this place better than anyone? Jerks!"

And then, it hits me--Jesus knew he was going to endure death on a cross for "these people." All people. Jesus died for jerks. I would have backed out. Jesus could have. But he didn't. I am convinced it was His choice to be obedient to the Father. Not just God laying a bound lamb on an altar. If you do not believe Jesus had the freedom to look around and into the future at the jerks he was doing this for and walk away, you have missed the beauty and significance of the Garden.

I cannot explain the power of this moment for me in the Garden and the impact of this realization. This truth penetrated my heart and the words "Jesus died for jerks" lingered in my mind for the rest of the trip. I mean, if Jesus died for jerks, I should at least change my attitude towards them. Right?

We left the Garden. Just outside the walls surrounding it were a couple of street vendors. These men were selling scarves out of the trunks of their cars, and I didn't think much of it. I continued to walk with our group, only to look back and see my wife Jena and two other ladies from the group had stopped to do some shopping. The rest of our group was heading up the road toward the city of Jerusalem.

I still remember I was wearing my bright reflective long sleeve running shirt so Jena could find me in a crowd. I don't run, unless I am chasing one of my kids or running down a pop fly in wiffleball. But running gear looks stylish and I feel healthier when I wear it. In addition, I knew there would be many crowded moments on this trip where I would need to be visible to Jena so we weren't separated.

Our group of fifty or so stopped, standing somewhat single file behind our guide halfway up the hill to Jerusalem. I'm standing at the end of our group when after about ten minutes, I realize that our entire group is waiting on my wife ...to buy a scarf! I trot back down to where my wife is negotiating with a street vendor, and I encourage her to make the purchase so we can get going. She then gives me this look of "Help me. I can't tell this guy 'no'."

Jena is holding several scarves in her hand, and I can tell she's holding them out so the vendor will take them back. But he's not taking them. I grab the scarves from Jena and try to force them back into the hands of the vendor. I tell him "Thank you, but we're going to keep looking."

He snaps. He slaps the scarves out of my hands and they scatter all over the ground. He begins yelling in his broken English, "What you want?! I give you a commission! This make you happy?!" It's a huge scene and now everyone in this crowded street is quiet and looking at us. It was awkward and I was embarrassed.

I think to myself, "What a jerk!"

And then, it hits me. Oh, I get it Lord. We're right outside of the Garden where you could have backed out of being obedient even unto death, but you didn't. You died for this guy. I guess the least I can do is be kind to him.

I get it.

But I didn't.

I grabbed Jena's hand, apologized again and headed to rejoin our group, winding our way through a sea of people, catching up with our group on the hill towards the old city of Jerusalem. I give our guide towards the top of the hill a wave signaling I've got the lost lamb so we can resume our walk to the Holy City.

Two things were happening that I wasn't aware of.

First, if you engage in any negotiation with a street vendor or shop owner for an extended period of time...you're committed. You are expected to make a purchase of some kind. To just walk away at this point is an incredible insult. This will only result in the vendor trying to save face at your expense. Usually in the form of increasing levels of public humiliation, until he gets the upper hand in his mind.

Secondly, if you are slightly taller than average, quasi-confident, and you're the only one wearing a bright reflective shirt in your group...you must be the guide! I didn't know that. I do now. This street vendor thought I was the guide directing my group away from his merchandise.

About five minutes later, this vendor is back in my face! He had weaseled in and out of a crowd of thousands of people, completely abandoning his car and merchandise. We are now chest-to-chest and he is pointing his finger in my face yelling, "You are the scum of the earth! Pig!" and some other stuff I didn't understand --I'm pretty sure I shouldn't repeat if I did.

Have you heard how when you are close to death your whole life passes in front of your eyes? I believe it's true. As this guy is at the peak of his rage, in a nanosecond, I imagine myself punching him in the face, me being arrested and then rotting in a Palestinian jail with my kids growing up without a dad.

That's what I saw. I didn't like where that ended up. So instead, with my finger now in his face, I firmly say, "Listen! I'm not a guide! This is my wife and you'd better back off!" To which he yelled something in Arabic and then finally started to walk away.

It was intense.

My blood was boiling.

I was ready to fight.

So, I do what any brave American husband would do in a similar situation. I changed my shirt. Seriously, it was way too easy for him to find me. And I looked over my shoulder the rest of the day.

And somewhere in the Holy Land that evening an Arab-Israeli goes home with one more scarf than he had hoped, sits down at the dinner table with his wife and kids and says, "You wouldn't believe what this one American did today. What a jerk!"

Yep, Jesus died for jerks. Just like me.

TAKEAWAY

Is there a current situation where you could extend a little more grace?

Where have you seen God's grace in your life?

18

• • •

The Carpenter
and a Cougar

*"[The Devil] prowls around like a roaring lion, looking
for someone to devour."*
— *The Apostle Peter, 1 Peter 5:8*

My dad started our family glass business when I was eight years
old. It wasn't long after I would find myself riding in the van to job
sites or being introduced to customers as "Daddy's helper." When I
was ten, I got my first serious cut that required stitches, a common
consequence of working in the glass business. I have eighteen scars
on my hands, one scar for each year I worked full time as a glazier.

During those years my dad would always keep a carpenter on staff
so we could handle some of the bigger commercial and residential
jobs requiring structural reconfiguration and finish trimming. From
the age of eighteen to twenty-two, I was the carpenter's apprentice.

I had some great teachers, as these men were some skilled
carpenters--men gifted in their trade and some of the best

problem-solvers I've ever known. I believe a pastor should be required to spend twelve years as a carpenter before going into ministry, kind of like Jesus did.

One of these carpenters was named Leonard. Always somewhat mysterious, he was 5'5' inches tall-ish, maybe 135 pounds with his tool belt on. How he kept his tool belt on was a mystery in itself because he didn't have a butt. I didn't ask but I assumed he had worked it off. How he kept his pants up was a miracle as well, and one I'm thankful for! Leonard was probably in his early sixties, but we don't really know. Despite his age he was as strong as an ox. I worked with Leonard when I was twenty-one, while I was in my prime. I've never been stronger, leaner or meaner than when I was in my early twenties, and Leonard could lift stuff by himself that I couldn't. It was like watching an ant moving something ten times its size. You'd see this big forty-eight inch steel door going toward the job site from the truck, and there would be little Leonard hefting it from below, like an ant carrying a huge leaf.

I loved working with Leonard. I loved a lot of things about him. Yes, I even loved the way he would answer his cell phone: "Yellow. This'slenerd." In honor of Leonard I still answer my phone with the occasional "Yellow." Our motto was "Nothing's ever easy." Almost every job seemed to be bigger than our estimator had figured. We would constantly run into something that required on-the-job-engineering, but he was a genius. Leonard built our family's cabin on the lake with nothing more than my dad's napkin drawing.

I say he was mysterious because his name was William, but he insisted we call him Leonard, without explanation. And we didn't really know where he came from or where he went when he quit working for us, which he did twice over a five-year span. He just came in one day and said, "I got to leave." No two-week notice. No reason. Just gone.

He was a quiet guy, like deep water. He didn't make a lot of noise, but when he spoke, he had something to say which came from a deep place of wisdom and experience. I had to ask tons of questions to draw information out of him. He never exaggerated. You could tell when he got mad because his face would turn deep red and he'd start grinding his teeth. He had probably been angry a lot before he came to our company because his top and bottom teeth, though a little jagged, lined up perfectly like two puzzle pieces. Leonard never yelled or threw anything. This was an attribute I welcomed considering the long line of carpenters I'd worked with in the past. The only history we really knew on Leonard was he told us he used to build log cabins and guide hunts in the Rocky Mountains. He hunted elk and mule deer but his specialty was cougar.

He told me stories about how he would track these cougars. Looking for prints, signs and scat, he could find where they would bed down, what tree they'd been in, and where they would perch to scope out their prey. In addition, he could tell what they had eaten for their last meal and how long ago they had been in the area. Leonard was a fascinating individual.

He told me how the cougar has this thumb claw above its front paws. He called it a "rip claw." He brought one in to work one day, having cut it off a cougar he had killed. It was razor sharp and was about two inches long and shaped like a letter "C." Thick at the bottom and tapering to a sharp point. He said, "When a cougar pounces on its prey, it's so efficient, so calculated, that in one fluid motion it can pin the deer or prey to the ground (and) at the same time running the rip claw across the jugular…bleeding it out for a quick kill and an easy meal."

He said his mother was half Native American, which was hard to imagine given his light complexion and blue eyes. Because he was good at tracking and he'd never had poison ivy, I believed his bloodline claim. He was so good at tracking, in fact, that on one occasion he said the local authorities called him to look for a missing person and to scout an area of the mountain range for cougar activity. He had the horrendous job of looking for clothing or remains from the individual. He said he found what they were looking for but, despite my pressing for more details, never told me what he'd found, saying it was "too gruesome." As my imagination tried to fill in the gaps--I visualized hiking shoes with feet still in them.

He did tell me one of the eeriest things he experienced was when he was scouting for cougar, and the process of following tracks and signs led him to where a cougar had been perched just at the base of the timberline. He could tell that the cougar had spent a lot of time hunting in this area and perhaps did a lot of stalking of prey from this point, including a knoll where the big cat had perched many times. As Leonard came up over the knoll, he expected to find a ranch or a farm. Instead, he found a playground connected to a grade school just a hundred yards below.

He took the school officials up there, and then, they paid him to track the cougar and "eliminate the threat." Leonard said, "As crafty as those cougars are, the only thing keeping this particular cougar from attacking a child must have been the presence of a teacher. Or the fact a child never strayed too far away from the group."

There is a phenomenon known to animal behavior researchers. To explain it you need to imagine a hundred huddled, grazing buffalo on the Dakota plains, moving slowly almost like a dark flat cloud across the ground. Off to the edge is a pack of wolves lounging around like pets, with wolf pups playing and nipping at each other. The alpha male is lying down like a hound dog on the front porch. Can you picture it?

When the alpha male jumps to attention, the rest of the pack takes notice of his reaction. The alpha has become aware of a new vulnerability in the herd called "The Gap." Wolves, lions, cheetahs... criminals...all predators recognize gaps. It happens when one of the animals strays just a little too far away from the safety of the herd. In these moments, the alpha wolf knows he can successfully feed his pack. If he can maximize or increase "The Gap," he will separate his prey even further from the herd, guaranteeing a kill.

I think about Leonard's cougar story when I read this passage in 1 Peter that says, "Stay alert! Watch out for your great enemy, the devil. He prowls around like a roaring lion, looking for someone to devour." If someone told us there was a mountain lion watching our children play, we would definitely do something about it. I'd go out there with my rifle and stand guard over my kids. I might even go cougar hunting like the school officials asked Leonard to do.

Why is it when God tells us we have an enemy like a hungry lion "looking for someone to devour," we seem to embrace a more passive approach? You and I share a common enemy: a hungry cougar that is looking for an ideal opportunity to pounce. He's looking for "The Gap." We would be wise to stay close to our teacher and carpenter, Jesus, lest we become an unwitting victim.

I don't even want to describe how we could become vulnerable to weakening of our relationship with God or family, with a loss of health or peace. But because the enemy prowls…looking for whom he can devour, we need to stay alert, close to the herd of fellow believers and our Good Shepherd, Jesus.

TAKEAWAY

Identify the gap. What are some ways you've strayed a little too far from Jesus recently?

Are there any cougar signs in your daily habits or relationships that would indicate the enemy is close and action is required?

19

• • •

Smells Like Smoke

"Even though I walk through the valley of the shadow of death, I will fear no evil, for you are with me"[27]. *—David the shepherd Psalm 23:4*

Does it ever feel like God is distant? I don't mean silent. That's different. My wife can be silent but if she is in the same room reading a book, there is still a level of intimacy in her nearness. Silence can actually be a part of God's character.

Does God ever feel distant? Absent?

Sometimes I'm jealous of the disciples. These guys hung out with Jesus, God in the flesh, for three years!

I can't prove this is true from scripture, but I think Jesus smelled like smoke. I imagine that Jesus and the disciples camped out a lot. And I picture them on a hillside near the Sea of Galilee and the campfire is roaring and all the disciples are just reminiscing the day as Jesus himself sits quietly with a gentle smile on his face. They talk about the miracles, the ministry, everything. Think of the constant amazement at what they just witnessed each day. I imagine they fall asleep as the fire slowly goes out.

Then I imagine Jesus was always the first one to wake up. He was the one stoking the fire, knocking the ashes off the coals and getting things ready for breakfast.

I have a few friends who heat their home with wood. Occasionally, they'll come up to me to say "hello," and I'll smell the smoke on their clothes, lingering from stoking their wood burners in the morning. I love that smell. Do you ever imagine Jesus was so close to the disciples they could smell the smoke on His clothes? I'll come in from burning brush on the farm and my wife will say in a disgusted tone, "Ugh, you smell like smoke." "No honey", I'll reply, "I smell like Jesus."

I'll bet Jesus would throw a few logs on the fire to get breakfast started. I can imagine Peter was probably the next one awake...and every morning for three years Peter would say... "Hey Jesus, what are we going to do today?" It's the question my son Evan asked me every morning until he was seven years old. "Hey Dad, what are we going to do today?" And six times out of seven, I would say, "Well son, I'm going to head into work." Then he would say, "What are we going to do when you get home?"

I love that! His question is not just a search for activity-- it's a pursuit of relationship. To hang out with the guy he loves the most, his dad. It's the world to him to know that his daddy is near. My son's question motivates me during the day. I look forward to getting home and spending time with him.

"Hey Jesus, what are we going to do today?" That question implies an adventure, a journey, a relationship.

Nearness.

You would never go up to a stranger and say, "Hey man, what are we going to do today?" That's weird. But if I called up a friend right now and asked that question, he would assume I had in mind those three things: adventure, a journey, our relationship.

The disciples were able to ask Jesus that question every day! God is near. Fully understanding that truth might just change things. I also understand that it is actually possible for some of us to not want to know this truth that "God is near."

Because to fully comprehend this truth changes things. It would have to.

To assume God is distant feels safer. It's comfortable. Think about it, to know God is near is risky. He might ask me to give something up. If He is near, I need to stop hanging out at certain places. If God is near, then I better be careful what I look at or what I watch. If God is near, he might ask me to forgive someone. If God is near, he might give me a tough assignment.

Sometimes I would rather treat God like cough syrup. You know, in the medicine cabinet somewhere...in the bathroom...on the second floor. When I have a cold or a cough I'll go digging for it. I'll take a swig of God twice a day until my cough is gone. God is just near...enough. When things are tough or someone we love, especially ourselves, is sick, we will actually go and search for God. We go looking for Him, and we'll return to church or even pick up the Bible and read a Proverb or two.

God, forgive us for treating you this way and for not wanting to know you as near.

I have some friends who told me about a vacation they took with their daughters when they were younger. Roger and Nancy said they were driving through Death Valley National Park. The place is hot and dry and holds the world record for hot—134 degrees! The road is narrow and Roger remembers following behind this old camper for miles and miles, just creeping along unable to pass. He said he finally prayed out loud, "Lord, if you're listening, please help us get by this camper." To everyone's amazement at that very moment the camper pulled over to let them by. As they passed they noticed that the driver was a man with long hair and long beard, and one of his daughters asked, "Daddy, is that Jesus?"

Now that's teaching your children God is near! So near, in fact, it's not completely out of the question to see him driving a camper through a national park. Roger and Nancy drove their daughters through Death Valley when they were little. They did a great job teaching their children that God is near.

And then, a few years ago they found themselves in another kind of valley. Their daughter Alissa was diagnosed with a rare form of cancer.

I had the privilege of helping honor her life and legacy at her memorial service. I can still remember looking out at Roger, Nancy and all Alissa's classmates. It hit me while standing at the podium... understanding this truth that God is near changes everything.

Even in death, as Christ followers we simply experience a new level of nearness with Jesus. I find a whole lot of hope in that. Without understanding God's proximity, his geography, it matters very little "who" he is.

To know that God is good means very little to us if we assume he is distant or distracted.

To know that God is generous, loving, strong, caring... means nothing if we think he is absent.

To know God is near, however, changes everything.

We don't have to understand it. We don't have to figure it out. It simply means we keep walking.

Keep trusting.

God is near.

Do you smell the smoke?

TAKEAWAY

Adventure. Journey. Relationship. Which of these three are missing in your relationship with Jesus today?

For the next seven days, start your morning with this question, "Hey Jesus, what are we going to do today?" Journal any ways you sense him answering this question.

20

• • •

Help Wanted

"God decided in advance to adopt us…"
- The Apostle Paul, Ephesians 1:5

While I was a student at Cedarville College in Ohio, I had to find a job. College is expensive. I was broke. My roommates were broke too. Since our schedules with sports didn't accommodate real jobs, we would honestly wake up some mornings and say, "What can we do today to make ten bucks?"

I remember several days we would grab buckets and rags and wash windows for the businesses in nearby towns. One dollar per pane per side. We would find out who the property owners were in town, and we would call them up and contract to paint their apartment buildings. I once made cookies and got our girlfriends to sell them to the guys who were studying for finals. A friend from our dorm taught us how to go to auctions and buy antiques to refinish and then sell them through the classifieds. We delivered phone books to an entire city for a nickel per book. We donated…uh, sold plasma. Anything but get a real job to make money. We were serial entrepreneurs.

One day I noticed a "help wanted" poster on one of the bulletin boards around campus. A local sheep farmer was looking for help during lambing season, and he was willing to pay minimum wage, which had just gone up to $4.25 from $3.80. This was huge!

I called him. He hired me. I loved it.

This farmer had about fifty ewes and two busy rams. For those who may not know, ewes are the female sheep. Rams are the boys.

These ewes were all due to give birth just before spring break. My job was to feed and water the sheep, early in the morning and then later in the afternoon after classes.

I'd occasionally clean out the stalls every other week or so. I loved being around the farm. I moved hay bales to the loft. I'd move sheep from the barn to the pasture.

However, after four weeks I began to realize something. I wasn't being paid. In addition, I was afraid to say anything because I really loved the work. Wouldn't we all love to find an employee like that?

Soon the birthing began. The farmer became anxious. He knew something I did not but was about to learn. Lambing was hard work. I don't know if you've seen the birth of farm animals, but it is one of the most disgusting and miraculous things you will ever witness.

I remember a day when one of the ewes was having trouble giving birth. The farmer got this concerned look on his face. We had just lost a ewe during the birthing process a few days earlier. He knew that with some of the difficulties that sheep experience, there was a chance we could lose both the ewe and the lamb. He said something about the lamb being backwards in the birth canal and that he needed to make an adjustment.

Next thing I witness, he rolls up his sleeves and, yep, sticks his hand and arm into the birth canal. He's trying to get the lamb turned front feet first, nose down. He brings his arm out...takes off his watch and says, "Hold this. I don't want to lose it." He goes back in.

If you could have seen me in this moment, you would have seen my eyes as big as saucers. I'm pretty sure the rams in the stall next to us had the same look on their faces.

The farmer makes the adjustment, pulls out his arm, and the lamb comes squirting out. The lamb is delivered. But it's not breathing. He takes the lamb and wipes away some of the afterbirth around the lamb's face and proceeds to try to give this lamb mouth-to-mouth resuscitation. He covers the lambs face with his mouth, and he's blowing, inflating the lungs. I watch the lamb's rib cage expand. He pulls away and I can see the lungs deflate. After a few minutes of this, the farmer stops. The lamb is dead. The farmer, undeterred, goes to Plan B.

In the stall next to us was an orphan lamb that was born a few days earlier, and its mother had died while giving birth. He took the orphaned lamb and tied his legs together so it couldn't walk. The farmer took the dead lamb and covered the living lamb with as much of the afterbirth as he could. And then, he put the orphaned lamb in the stall with the ewe that had just about swallowed the farmer's watch moments ago. We hoped the ewe would adopt the orphaned lamb as hers. She did.

While wiping his hands off with a towel, not even turning to look at me, he said matter of fact, "Hey, if I'm not here for some reason…you may need to do that."

At which point I thought it was a good time to bring up the fact that I hadn't even been paid yet.

Something happened to me during that short lambing season. I fell in love with the farm. Today we have sheep on our own farm. I've had to do all the details described in this story, …and more. Now my kids look at me with the same big-eyed look I had more than twenty years ago. I often tell people if I could make a living losing money, I'd make a great farmer. While I've almost figured out how to break even, I've resigned to embrace the valuable lessons that can be learned from these sheep every day. Lessons like hard work, gains, losses, and orphan lambs covered with the blood of a lamb that died.

Jesus did that for us. We were orphans. Adopted. Covered by Jesus' blood. Purchased with full inheritance rights as a child of God.

"In love, [God] predestined us for adoption to himself as sons through Jesus Christ...In him we have redemption through his blood, the forgiveness of our [sins], according to the riches of his grace, which he [smears all over] us... In him we have obtained an inheritance...." [28]

Adoption awaits. It's your choice.

TAKEAWAY

Have you accepted the gift of God's adoption into His family?

If so, find time this week and write/tell/record your story. Share it with someone you care about or needs to hear it.

If not, would you want to join God's family today? You can pray something like this...

God, I admit that I'm a sinner. An orphan in need of a family. I believe you sent Jesus to die for my sins. I believe his blood has purchased me. I confess that Jesus Christ is Lord, and I believe in my heart that You raised him from the dead. From this day forward, you're the boss. In Jesus' name, Amen.

21

• • •

Your Turn

"...In the future your children will ask you, 'What do these stones mean?' Then you can tell them..."
— *Joshua 4:6-7*

When asked what the world would look like in a hundred years, author and speaker Anne Lamott replied, "The next hundred years? All new people."[29]

Do a little math. If all your children had three kids and those grandkids had three kids, and then your great grandkids all had three kids, how many would come behind you just on your branch of the family tree in the next hundred years? To make it easier take the number of kids you have or hope to have and multiply by forty. What's your number?

For those who are reading who maybe are unable to have children or have chosen not to, let me say, your influence on those that come behind you in the next hundred years will be just as significant. Your story is so important and needs to be shared.

280. Two...Eight...Zero.

This is my number. No, we don't know what that number will actually be. Could be less. Could be more. Nevertheless, this book is for them. Stories about their father, grandfather and great-grandfather that simply point them to a better story.

Every time I sit in a movie theater and watch the previews for the movies "coming soon," there are at least one or two previews that cause me to shake my head and lean towards my wife and whisper, "The world is desperate for better stories."

This is where you come in. Will you tell your "And then..."?

I remember hearing a story about a young couple dating in the early 1970's. The Vietnam War was coming to an end and he had just finished his basic training. She was in high school. They were both Christ followers believing God had a plan for their lives.

And then, she found out she was pregnant. With fear of the disappointment and hurt her parents would feel, they met first with her pastor and shared their situation. With his encouragement and council, they spoke with her mother and father. And yes, they were met with many emotions. There was much discussion of the choices they had before them.

For one, her father had just been promoted by his company and the family would be moving in just a few months from their small town to a large city out west. They talked about making the move sooner. No one would know their situation and possibly they could avoid some embarrassment.

In less than a year the US Supreme Court would rule on Roe v. Wade, making it legal to abort a pregnancy anywhere in America with only a few stipulations. In the back of their minds, they knew the option of abortion would be available in the new city.

Thankfully, the small-town doctor kindly advised, "You don't want to make that choice." Not to avoid embarrassment or shame. Not even for lost dreams. There was so much potential for this couple. If only they could be spared the burden of raising a child at such a young age. But the couple felt strongly in their hearts that their wrong choices should not lead to another.

Instead of embracing a "The end," they began to unpack what it would look like to process an "And then...". They chose to allow God to pick up the pieces and make a family that would honor Him.

There was a wedding and they began their young lives as a married couple with a baby on the way. It wasn't an easy path and the road had twists and turns but God was faithful in the journey. Choosing an "And then..." gives God permission to keep writing. Almost fifty years later their story continues.

If you could sit across the table from this couple and have a cup of coffee with them, I know what they would tell you. They would say, "Do not embrace a 'The end' where God wants to write an 'And then....'"

I know that is what they would tell you because that is what they have been telling me for the last forty years. I was that baby who was born a few weeks after my mom's seventeenth birthday.

My parents are some of the bravest, most generous people I know. I've had a front row seat as I've watched God bless them. I've watched how God has blessed their ministry as leaders in our community. Their kingdom impact could not be tallied even yet.

But here is where the battle began for me. When I was in fifth grade, my dad and I sat in the back room of the Pizza House restaurant in Galesburg, Illinois at a table for two with a pepperoni and black olive pizza between us. He said, in a moment of incredible honesty and humility... "Hey son, you're learning about the birds and the bees at school...and um...it's not going to take long for you to figure out the math on the difference between our wedding date and your birthday. You'll discover your mom and I made a mistake...."

Looking back, I think, I wouldn't have figured the math out till I was in my thirties!

What my dad said was, "Your mom and I made a mistake." His desire and prayer for me was purity until marriage.

Nevertheless, when dad said, "We made a mistake...", I heard,

"You're a mistake." And the enemy said, "You're an accident, you were never planned. God can't have a plan for you."

That was a lie.

I believed it.

You may have to go back to when you were in fifth grade to recognize when your battle began. For me, it was a lie I believed through my teen years, into college, into early adult life. When something would happen, and I would make a mistake in school or business or marriage or, like in the youth service where my pants ripped and I embarrassed myself, I would make a vow. "I'll never speak in public again. I'll never try that again. It doesn't matter--I'm an accident. I'm worthless."

Or, at least, worth...less.

Do you see the potential generational baggage that could be carried into so many branches of your family tree if someone, somewhere along the line doesn't embrace the truth of a God who loves to write "And then..." into our stories? It's devastating. Marriages, families, careers and more have been causalities of this war between "And then..." and "The end."

There are people reading this thinking, "But you don't know what I've done. Even if I could get my life together, God wouldn't want it." Maybe you say, "I was in a similar situation and I chose differently. I had the abortion. I keep giving in to the same addiction. I've messed up so bad I can't forgive myself. How can God?" It's "The end" for me.

This is the battle. Do you see it? You're losing the battle for your heart. You've settled for a "The end." You're owning a future for your heart that contradicts God's heart for your future. You've bought the lie that somehow you are "worth...less."

You may have messed up so bad the world can actually say you are "worthless." In fact, the church may be able to say it.

God says you are worth more.

I am amazed at how my kids will stare at the screens on their phones all day. It drives me crazy! What are they doing? Most of the time, they are watching and listening to other people's stories. Funny, crude, inappropriate…rarely inspiring and beneficial. However, each of them will look up from their screens and listen to their grandpa or grandma tell a story. I love that. I do not want to be remembered by my kids for constantly yelling at them to get off their phones. I want to give them a better option. I want to engage them with better stories.

Want to inspire your kids? Tell a better story.

Want to motivate your team? Tell a better story.

Want customers to choose your business? Tell a better story.

Want to leave a legacy? Tell a better story.

Want to change the world? Tell a better story.

My wife and I went for coffee this afternoon. We ran into a friend whose mother has dementia. She was on her way to visit the nursing home where her mom resides. She was telling us how grateful she was that a few years back she and her husband gave her grandma a tape recorder and told her if she ever thought of a story to push "record" and tell it. Now, grandma is gone. Our friend is amazed at how her mother lights up at the sound of her mother's voice. Not to mention how much she herself is learning about her own family history.

I love that! I promise you those cassette tapes that cost $1.89 at Wally World will become priceless over time.

Speaking in public used to be my number one fear in life. Sometimes I think it still is. We attended a church many years ago, and the young man doing announcements was terrible. He seemed nervous and unprepared. He was monotone and didn't reflect the excellence we witnessed everywhere else in the church. As an attender in the back row, scared to death of public speaking, I found myself thinking, "I could do better than this guy!" And a few years later, I was asked to do just that.

If mediocrity can inspire you, so be it!

My prayer for this book is not to sell ten thousand copies. Rather, my prayer is for a few of you to finish it and say, "I can do better than this!" If that's you, let me say this, "You are right!" Sit down at your computer and begin to type, grab a journal and start writing, or flip on the microphone and begin to record and share your stories.

Mark Batterson has said, "Everyone has at least one book in them."[30] I believe him. This is mine.

Now it's your turn.

Do it.

Tell the story of when you failed or how you won. Make us laugh or make us cry. Fiction or non-fiction or both.

Write the script.

Shoot the film.

Compose the song.

Tell a story.

The world is desperate for better stories.

This is not "The end." This is the beginning of your "And then".

Never stop sharing stories.

Epilogue

"A good book has no ending." – *RD Cumming*

While I pray that you have finished reading this book with a deep conviction for sharing your stories, I have one final admonition: Develop an authentic curiosity for other's stories.

When my youngest daughter was just learning to talk we would catch her mimicking the story tellers in our home. With all the verbal inflection and body language of someone with an important story to share she would seize the lull in the conversation and grab the spotlight unleashing her monologue of gibberish. We thought it was hilarious. Our smiles and laughter only fueled her energetic standup routine. We thought it was so cute and funny, we didn't want it to stop...sometimes. When she was finished with all of the verbal intonation of a grand conclusion, one of us would say, "Really?". "Yeah!", was her reply with a big smile.

"And then what happened?", I would ask. She would look around the room a little puzzled for a moment, and then, realizing it was a chance to continue her story, would jump right back into it repeating some of the same familiar gibberish we had just heard.

Here's a storytelling tip: If you want others to listen to the stories you share, you'll need to develop authentic curiosity and desire to listen to other's stories.

We all know that one guy...that dominates every gathering with the same stories. Don't be that guy. Don't be the person who talks so much that when you finally have something to share, no one is listening.

Focus first on being tactfully curious. I'm not sure who said it first, but it's true: nobody cares how much you know until they know how much you care.

The other day as I was driving, I saw a man driving his electric wheel chair down the side walk. He was missing both legs below the knees. A small American flag flew from a pole on the back of his scooter about three feet above his head. I'd guess him to be in his late sixties.

I'm genuinely curious. He has a story. I've seen him downtown at a certain gas station buying coffee. If I get the chance, I'll buy his coffee and introduce myself. It may not happen on the first meeting, but I'll tactfully be looking for a chance to say, "Tell me your story."

Several months ago, while sitting in a tree stand during bow season, I made a list. "The top ten people who have most influenced my life", I wrote at the top of the back of a receipt I found in my pocket. Professors, coaches, pastors, friends, authors, neighbors, and family members. Some of them didn't know me. I've been influenced by them from the back row of a lecture hall or a sanctuary. I sent them each a card thanking them for the impact they've had on my life. I tried to be specific about the sermon or lesson and how it created a change in my thinking. At the bottom I offered to buy them a cup of coffee at their convenience. I closed with my cell number.

"Hey Scott. I received your gracious card. Thanks for the kind words. Would be happy to meet you", came one text reply. "This is John by the way."

If you get the chance to connect with the people who have impacted you the most in your life, you'll discover, like I did... they're authentically curious. You'll find they ask more questions than you. So be intentional.

The lady at the crosswalk in front of the school that helps kids across the street before school.

The guy that picks up trash in the terrace in front of the grocery store.

The old couple that sits on the dock at the lake.

The barista, your barber, your mechanic, and the farmer.

Your grandma, your dad, your daughter, and your grandson.

They have a story too.

Develop a tactful, authentic curiosity for other's stories.

I'd love to hear the story of how this book has impacted you. You can reach me at scott@scottanthonycramer.com or give me call at 309-297-0637.

Family Study

These chapters are designed to be short and attention grabbing for all ages. Consider reading a chapter a few times a week after dinner or another time with the family gathered. Follow up with these questions. Or, better yet, read the chapter to get the point being made and write and read your own story using the following questions as a guide for your discussion.

Chapter 1 – And Then... page 1
1. There is power in a story. What is your favorite movie or book? Why?
2. Can you think of an example where a story motivated you to make a change or take action?

Chapter 2 – 90 Seconds page 11
1. Take a moment and list some people, experiences or things you are thankful for. For what are you hopeful? Why these?
2. Have you ever experienced this special 90-second moment? How does it affect your life? Was it what you expected? Why or why not?
3. What story can you tell or share about this special moment? Hint: build your story with rich description, having a beginning, middle and end to help visualize this 90-second moment.

4. What distractions are keeping you from living your life in this 90-second space between thankful and hopeful? What Bible verses will help you live more thankful and hopeful?

Chapter 3 – Sweet Silence page 19

1. Read these two verses then explain how you know God hears your prayers, even when you feel He is silent: "I love the Lord because he hears my voice and my prayer for mercy," and "The Lord is far from the wicked, but he hears the prayers of the righteous."
2. Have you ever sensed God's silence in response to your prayers at a critical time, as Mary and Martha did? What happened? If there was there an "And then…" moment when you trusted His silence, explain how and what happened next.
3. In which prayer concerns do you feel like you're waiting for God to respond in your life right now? How does this chapter encourage you?
4. How does it change things if you knew God was trusting you with His silence? Tell/write/record your personal "And then…" moment when your faith grows stronger in His silence.

Chapter 4 – Road Kill page 23

1. Retell the story of the turtle in your own words. Would you have gone back to help him, like Scott did? Why or why not?
2. What life experience were you reminded of in this story about the turtle?
3. Describe a dream you've perhaps allowed to die on the roadside of life. What is one thing you could do today that would be a step toward breathing life back into that crushed dream? Explain how an "And then…" moment could change everything.
4. Who could you encourage today with writing/telling/recording this story or one of your own in which you brought life back into something that appeared lost?

Chapter 5 – Sparkle page 26

1. Describe some examples of things that make your eyes sparkle.
2. What are some things you've been carrying that have stolen your sparkle? What lesson from this story can help you get it back? Has something happened in life that didn't turn out the way you expected? What? How would Philippians 4:7 help you handle it with God's peace?
3. What can you do to hear from God every day?
4. Write/tell/record a story that would be an encouragement to someone else who may be struggling with peace after a tragedy. Did your story help someone flip a "Then end" into an "And then…"?

Chapter 6 – Imaginary Sharks page 32

1. Explain what Scott means by a "shark" in someone's life. Do you have one?
2. Identify the imaginary sharks in your life right now that are stealing your peace. How are they alike/different from threats by real sharks?
3. What would it look like to allow Jesus to hold your hand when you experience fears? What Bible verses would you cling to? Explain how your heavenly Father's presence, promise and power can make a difference in dealing with fears.
4. Write/tell/record your story of a specific time when Jesus's presence, promise and power turned fear into peace with an "And then…" moment.

Chapter 7 – Creekin' Shoes page 39

1. Scott explains how God turns around someone's life who has a kind of fatigue in resisting temptation. Put the last paragraph in this chapter in your own words, inserting your name before "creekin' shoes."
2. How can you trust God to use an imperfect you to impact the world?

3. Is there anywhere you have settled for "creekin' shoe faith" in your life, somewhere you have given up in resisting temptation? Are you embracing a future for your heart that contradicts God's heart for your future? Explain how this verse compares with your experience: "This means that anyone who belongs to Christ has become a new person."

4. Has there been an "And then..." moment in your life when you experienced God's greatest work after you've given in to temptation? Write/tell/record this story and share it with someone.

Chapter 8 – Thin Ice page 42

1. Interview a parent/grandparent/relative who has had many life experiences. Write/tell/record their story, highlighting the wisdom and insights you personally gain from learning of risks taken and advice heeded or NOT!

2. Describe your emotions as you read Scott's story, especially how you felt as he fell through the ice and clambered up the bank. Put yourself in his place--what circumstance would have been the most challenging for you? Why?

3. "Thin ice" is also a metaphor for risky decisions we make without heeding common sense or good advice, right?! Has there been a time when you could look back on a decision that ended poorly and think, "How could I not have seen that coming?" Why did you not anticipate what happened next? Did someone try to warn you? Explain.

4. Write/tell/record what you learned from this failure to get or take advice and what wisdom would you pass on to the next generation from that experience.

Chapter 9 – Bait, Beans & Bells page 48

1. Take a few minutes and thank God for all the ways he's provided for you in the past. What comes to your mind first? Why do you think so?

2. Like Scott and his brother, have you ever prayed and waited for God to provide? What happened? Write/tell/record how God blessed.
3. Who in your life would be encouraged by your story? Prayerfully find a way to bless them.
4. In what areas in your life are you currently waiting for God's provision? How can this verse encourage you to pray and have hope? "And if God cares so wonderfully for flowers that are here today and thrown into the fire tomorrow, he will certainly care for you. Why do you have so little faith?"

Chapter 10 – Kayak Envy page 53
1. Ask at least one family member to describe how God helps them to be content. Perhaps ask them how they are thankful for YOU.
2. Take a moment and list three things you're thankful for that money cannot buy.
3. How has comparison in your life over possessions led to envy? Where has envy blinded you to God's blessings? How can we avoid constantly thinking we are missing something?
4. Write/tell/record about a time when God helped you be thankful for what you have.

Chapter 11 – Ripped Pants page 57
1. If you have not yet experienced the kind of pressure Scott writes about, write/tell/record Scott's story in your own words and share it.
2. Can you recall a past failure or embarrassment where, under intense pressure, you made a vow or promise? What were the circumstances? What happened? Did you keep the promise? Why or why not? Is this a promise you should or should not keep?
3. What lie is the enemy pressuring you to believe now? Based on Scott's story, how should you pray about it?

4. What if the enemy's greatest battle for your heart is an indication of where God wants to use you? What can you do about it? Write/tell/record this story and share.

Chapter 12 – Peter's Casting Call page 63

1. Write/tell/record any "And then..." moment of when you or someone in your family turned around a painful experience like Peter caused and allowed Jesus to heal. Share with someone who is hurting.
2. What could you do today to help those individuals look to Jesus as the one who reattaches ears?
3. Describe a situation in which someone may have "cut your ear off"? How did you respond? How would this story about Peter help you look to Jesus for healing?
4. Who are some of the people in your life who have suffered at the expense of your passionate "sword-swinging" in the name of Jesus? Where do you think your reasons for hurting people is coming from? Explain.

Chapter 13 – Help Me Love You page 66

2. Interview one of your teachers or grandparents, asking them to tell you of a time when God helped them to love someone they had previously thought unlovable. Write/tell/record this story and share it.
3. Retell Scott's "And then..." moment from your own perspective. Put yourself in his chair...how would your story change as you respond to Ann's insights?
4. Who in your life is hard to love? How can you love him/her the way God loves you?
5. Write/tell/record about a relationship that would be changed by loving someone the way God loves you.

Chapter 14 – Tie Some Shoes page 69
1. Did Scott's story end the way you predicted? Why or why not? Describe his "And then..." moment in your own words.
2. What are some ways you can "tie some shoes" for someone you typically would like to avoid? Would you be willing? Why or why not?
3. Have you ever had an experience similar to Scott's? If so, write/tell/record what happened and how you overcame the challenges of pride or lack of love.
4. Write/tell/record your commitment today to being ready for the opportunities to be like Jesus to those whom you come in contact with.

Chapter 15 – Greater Love page 73
1. Write/tell/record either Scott's story or one of your own to someone younger than you are, encouraging them to love those who may not love us back, just like Jesus does.
2. Describe any current relationships that are pretty much one-sided. How are you coping?
3. Explain how the verses in Scott's story may either inspire or discourage someone who is struggling to demonstrate unconditional, one-sided love.
4. What are some tangible ways we can allow this "greater love" to transform our relationships today?

Chapter 16 – Just You page 79
1. What does "following Jesus" mean to you? Explain, using Jesus' story in Mark. If you are unsure, ask people in your family or church. Write/tell/record their responses.
2. Find the "And then..." moment for the rich young ruler and paraphrase his story in your own words, including his response to Jesus' answer to his question in Mark 10:22.
3. Have you done what Jesus tells the rich young ruler and put Him first? If not, describe how your life would be different if you put

Him first. What are the "riches" in your life that may be keeping you from following Jesus?

4. Write/tell/record your story of deciding to follow Jesus, to having faith in him and to being one of his disciples. Why or how did you respond to His calling "just you"? Describe the impact this has had on your life today.

Chapter 17 – Jesus Died for Jerks page 85

1. When you say, "jerks," what do you really mean? Why do you think you respond that way? What options do you have?
2. In school, work or family, is there a current situation where you could extend a little more grace to someone else who needs it? What scripture would equip you to deal with "jerks"?
3. Describe a time when you needed to experience grace like Scott did. What happened? Did you have an "And then..." moment? How would Scott's experience in Israel help you see the truth of "Jesus died for jerks"?
4. Describe a past situation where God gave you just the kind of grace you needed to help another. If possible, write/tell/record this story and share with someone who would be blessed by how this experience increased your appreciation of Christ's willing sacrifice on the cross.

Chapter 18 – The Carpenter and a Cougar page 90

1. Imagine you had been a student or a teacher at the school in Scott's story. Compare how you felt being in the playground before and after Leonard killed the cougar. What life lesson did you learn?
2. Explain the significance of Leonard's story about the cougar near the school. How would you re-tell this story to those in your family or circle of friends? Could you include the verse from 1 Peter 5:8 to help apply the story's spiritual truth to your own life?

3. Identify a potential "gap" in your life. What are some ways you may have strayed a little too far from Jesus or the "herd" in your life? Are there any "cougar signs" in your daily habits or relationships that would indicate the enemy is close and action is required to stay safe? How can you return to the safety of the Good Shepherd?
4. Tell/write/record a story from your own life that resonates with Scott's. Be sure to include the "and then…" as well as any "cougar signs" leading up to your getting rid of or distancing yourself from the enemy and how your life is different now.

Chapter 19 – Smells Like Smoke page 95
1. Describe/retell Scott's "And then…" as he connects the camping story to knowing God's nearness changes everything.
2. Adventure. Journey. Relationship. Which of these aspects are missing in your relationship with Jesus today? Which Bible verses tell you how much God loves you? (yea though I walk, crucified with Christ, nevertheless I live, Christ in me…"
3. For the next seven days, start your morning with this question: "Hey Jesus, what are we going to do today?" Journal any ways you anticipate Him answering this question.
4. For seven more days, journal what happens during your day as you sense God's nearness. Write/tell/record how this kind of confident knowing changes your outlook and life.

Chapter 20 – Help Wanted page 99
1. Have you accepted the gift of God's adoption into His family?
2. If so, find time this week and write/tell/record your story. Share it with someone you care about or needs to hear it. Be sure to use "And then…" at the turning point in your life when you decided to follow Christ.
3. If not, would you want to join God's family today? You can pray something like this…

God, I admit that I'm a sinner. An orphan in need of a family. I believe you sent Jesus to die for my sins. I believe his blood has purchased me. I confess that Jesus Christ is Lord, and I believe in my heart that You raised him from the dead. From this day forward, you're the boss. In Jesus' name, Amen.

4. If this is your prayer, then go tell someone. If you're not sure who, contact Scott at scottacramer@icloud.com and he will help you make a connection.

Chapter 21 – Your Turn page 103

As you finish writing your story here are some venues to consider:

- Self- publish for free at createspace.com.
- Self- publish for a fee at Westbowpress.com
- Book cover art at 99designs.com
- Blog at wordpress.com

Notes

Unless otherwise noted, all scripture is from the Holy Bible, NLT New Living Translation, copyright © 1996, 2004, 2015 by Tyndale House Foundation. Used by permission of Tyndale House Publishers, Inc., Carol Stream, Illinois 60188. All rights reserved.

Scripture quotations marked (NIV) are taken from the Holy Bible, New International Version®, NIV®. Copyright © 1973, 1978, 1984, 2011 by Biblica, Inc.™ Used by permission of Zondervan. All rights reserved worldwide. www.zondervan.com The "NIV" and "New International Version" are trademarks registered in the United States Patent and Trademark Office by Biblica, Inc.™

1   Psalm 51:10a
2   "Top 25 Quotes by Erwin McManus (of 116)." A-Z Quotes. Accessed July 02 2018." http://www.azquotes.com/author/9888-Erwinn_McManus
3   David and Bathsheba's baby dies at birth, the nation of Israel suffers tremendously and eventually is divided into northern and southern kingdoms.
4   Matthew 1:1-17
5   McManus
6   My paraphrase
7   Lewis B. Swedes. Quotesabout.us accessed July 02, 2018 Keeping Hope Alive
8   Philippians 4:6-7 My paraphrase
9   Psalm 4:8 NIV
10 Philippians 4:19 NIV

11 Timothy 6:6b My paraphrase

12 Luke 22:49b

13 Matthew 26:35

14 Matthew 26:74

15 Mathew 26:75

16 And then…moment for Peter in Mark 17

17 Mark Batterson, sermon. April 6, 2014, Don't Judge Jonah

18 Proverbs 3:34 my paraphrase

19 John 15:13 NIV

20 Romans 5:8 KJV

21 My paraphrase

22 Mark 10:21b

23 Matthew 20:16

24 Luke 7:34

25 Matthew 11:11-18

26 Matthew 16:18

27 My Paraphrase

28 Ephesians 1:5

29 Anne Lamott. "Quotes from Anne Lommott" A-Z quotes azquotes.com/
    quote/456641

30 Mark Batterson, the Xulon Experience, March 20, 2014

Appendix

10 things to make your story unforgettable

	Before you write/tell/record… Determine the 5 W's and 2 H's to include as you develop details of your story: • Who is key in your story? • What interesting thing(s) happens to you or them? • When does this happen? • Where does it happen? • Why/how does it happen? • How did you or they experience spiritual insights or truth? • How can someone else learn from and spiritually connect to your story?
Having a catchy title makes people want to know more—and also hints at story's focus	**Trash or Treasure**

Create a setting, one with enough descriptive details for people to visualize	When I was just a kid, we moved into an old two-story house on Bateman St. in Galesburg, Ill. This house came complete with a big back yard, a concrete slab with two basketball hoops, a tether ball pole and enough room for Wiffle ball. Add to that the never-ending supply of garter snakes found under every rock and log, and this place was heaven for an 8-year-old.
Add characters to your story, but select only key ones that will add context	In addition, my dad built us a clubhouse behind the garage out of old pallets and scrap pieces of plexiglass from the glass company he was starting in the basement of this big old house. My brother and I loved to play army and pretend like we were cowboys with our cap guns.
Build interesting details in your story—do a show and tell for your readers/listeners to really hook them into staying with you to the end	One of the things I'll never forget was the treasure we found buried in the back yard. We didn't have to dig very deep in this one spot to find an old pocket watch frame with the face broken out. The next day I found an old metal tin soldier with his gun snapped off. Not long after, a pair of wire rim glasses with no lenses. A pirate's fortune for my brother and me. I would take these new found prized possessions and put them in an old King Edwards cigar box so no one could steal them. This was my treasure now.

Introduce conflict to story—as in this story: not treasure hunting but weed pulling	It was the first spring after we moved there that dad and mom planted our garden in our back yard...right over the X on my treasure map! Green beans, snap peas, strawberries were just a few of the things we grew. Now instead of digging for treasure, I spent my time digging up weeds! The soil was black, rich and soft. Certainly the most fertile soil on our property for a garden. The most fertile soil for weeds too, but it felt like everyday to the kid under 10--pull weeds in the garden, pull weeds in the rock driveway. Man, I'd pull weeds until my fingertips hurt.
Include lessons gained from looking back, dealing with original conflict— honestly and openly	I discovered later in my teenage years there was a reason this area of ground was so fertile. Back in the old days, 100 years ago...apparently there weren't garbage men and garbage trucks to come and pick up the garbage. So homeowners had burn piles, a spot in the back yard they would go and burn their trash.
Echo story focus and tie into meaning of story title. Build bridges with human experience.	What I thought was treasure...was actually trash! Someone's leftover trash from their burn pile. What I placed so carefully in a cigar box under my bed in hopes that no one would find it was someone's garbage!

Turning point-- connect insights from past situation to readers' potential current situation	I think we still do that sometimes. Even as a grown up…some of the things I hold on to the tightest are just garbage in the light of eternity. Jet Ski's, expensive clothes, cool phones and the latest toys will all be someone else's garbage to deal with in a hundred years or less. There is nothing wrong with these things. We just need to hold on to these things a little looser. And then…there are certain seasons of life that feel pretty trashy. We lose our job, we drop the ball, we blow it, we fail the test, someone we love hurts us with their words…someone we trust betrays us. Difficult seasons. Seasons that feel kinda trashy.
Turning point— broaden application to connect to spiritual truths	I wonder if when these "trashy" feeling things happen in our life, they are the very seasons that create the fertile soil God needs to grow the most beautiful fruit of our lives. Seasons that feel dead and spoiled…like trash providing nutrients to ground. Seasons that prick the heart…kind of like tilling soil. Sure there are some weeds we'll need to pull. Weeds love fertile soil too, and if we aren't diligent, we can allow sin and bitterness to take root and take over in the very places of our hearts that God wants to cultivate new fruit.

Conclusion—Be personal, be real, stay focused on the story's main idea. Tie up the loose ends: use your own personal experience to inspire others to aim to live in greater truth about God. Keep it brief.	I think if there is one place the enemy likes to get us stuck, it's in the definitions of trash and treasure. God wants to flip the trash. He doesn't want us to place too much value in the things the world calls treasure. Allow God to till the soil. You pull the weeds.

About the Author

Scott Cramer comes from a long line of story tellers. With almost a decade of full time ministry under his belt he's discovered the importance of telling better stories. Having witnessed first hand the impact of great communicators, Scott is now considered by many a master of developing a compelling story. Scott and his wife Jena and their seven children live on a hobby farm in Knox County, IL. For more information about Scott or additional resources to help you share your story, visit ScottAnthonyCramer.com.

CPSIA information can be obtained
at www.ICGtesting.com
Printed in the USA
LVHW111751031019
632932LV00007B/6/P

9 781973 644835